M000085589

# EVEN LOVE IS
# ODD

Ah, Love!

*Shirley Bahlmann*

# EVEN LOVE IS
# ODD

## TRUE OLD FASHIONED PIONEER
## STORIES OF LOVE AND ROMANCE

BY

SHIRLEY BAHLMANN

ASPEN
BOOKS

Bountiful, Utah

Even Love Is Odd
True Old Fashioned Pioneer Stories of Love And Romance:
Copyright 2002 Shirley Bahlmann
All rights reserved.

Distributed by Brigham Distributing
435-723-6611

Aspen Books, www.aboutaspenbooks.com

Printed in the United States of America
Grayson Printing, Spanish Fork, UT
10 9 8 7 6 5 4 3 2 1

Book design by Jeanette Andrews

ISBN:   1-56236-455-3

# DISCLAIMER

The author has made every effort to report the facts correctly as far as her research showed. It is interesting to note that even in separate accounts of the same incident, the "facts" are sometimes reported differently, depending on the point of view of the person telling the story. In one of these stories, the last name was shown with two different spellings, so I had to turn to the genealogy file and make my best educated guess!

At times I have found different stories that go so well together, I have taken the liberty of combining them for a richer reading experience.

The author sincerely hopes that all who are related to the people in these stories will enjoy these accounts and find them to be at least close to the traditions that are passed down from generation to generation.

# ACKNOWLEDGEMENTS

Thanks to Jani Masco for discovering the title for this book on a piece of my scrap paper and bringing it to my attention, to Dawna Vee Bown for her famous radio ad and her smart and savvy business sense, to Sue Beus for parking and pictures, to Candy Carmody for child care, and to my sweet and spunky ever-lovin' sister Loraine for her bullseye advice on matters of the heart!

My enduring thanks and love to my proofreaders; Bob, Andy, and Scott Bahlmann, Judy Gubler, Lannette Nielson, Linda Pratt, and Judi Hansen.

Thanks also to LoDel Beal and Carolyn Bessey for one-sided paper, and to Father in Heaven for absolutely everything!

# DEDICATION

To my little sister Carolyn, who is fulfilling her pre-mortal assignment to travel this life with a child's mind in an adult body. She often dreams of romance, marriage, and family. I know she'll find them someday.

# TABLE OF CONTENTS

# FOREWORD

I am captivated by studies that show the need for love as second only to the need for food and shelter. The intriguing force of love in our lives can work for our good or ill, for our ecstasy or our embarrassment. Some of the stories in this volume will tweak your funny bone, and some will touch your heart. Some are ultimately triumphant, and some end in disappointment. Some of the stories that I came across happened shortly after the turn of the 20th Century and just begged to be told, so along with love stories from the 1800's will be a few unforgettable dealings of the heart from the early 1900's. After all, when it comes to falling in love, aren't we all pioneers?

My first two books, "Against All Odds," and "Isn't That Odd?" were told from juvenile viewpoints, as children have such fresh perspectives and are easily able to say just what they feel. In writing these stories of romance, I found that a child's perspective couldn't engage the heart like the point of view of one of the people who was actually involved in the relationship. There are a few accounts from lookers on, but most of these stories are told from someone who actually sits at the heart of the matter.

So now curl up with someone you love (pets count), a box of tissues, and prepare to enjoy your foray through the foibles of love and romance.

# RAIN BARREL ROMANCE

When I looked in the mirror I didn't even recognize myself. I could hardly believe that the Goddess of Liberty in the flowing white robe looking back at me was really plain old Frederikke Tollestrup from small town Gunnison.

"Oh, Rikky, you look like a real princess!" my friend Amelia said, her hands clasped under her chin.

I turned away from the mirror to face her. "It should have been you," I blurted before I could stop myself. "They should have picked you. After all, you live here in American Fork. I'm just visiting for the summer."

Amelia raised her hands with her palms out toward me. "Oh, no. If you tried to get me up on that float in front of all those people, I'd die of fright and roll off right onto the street." She shrugged her shoulders. "I'd ruin the whole parade. You're the perfect Goddess, Rikky, and besides, you look even older than sixteen. You look like a real lady."

I turned back to the mirror and secretly admired the pink flush that crept into my cheeks from Amelia's praise. My hair had been twisted and pinned into blonde waves that curled around my Goddess of Liberty crown.

Amelia's father called out, "Time to go, ladies." I felt like I was walking on clouds as we made our way outside and Amelia's father helped me climb up onto the float. There was a narrow wooden rail bolted to the wagon bed for me to lean against so I could keep my balance as we rolled down the street. I didn't have a free hand to hold on with because I needed one hand to hold the liberty torch, and the other to wave at the crowds that lined both sides of the street.

I couldn't stop smiling as I greeted all the people who cheered and clapped when they saw me moving past. My float was right behind a wagon full of children dressed in old-fashioned pioneer clothes. Some of the little girls waggled their fingers shyly at me as they peeked at me from under their broad bonnets.

1

The idyllic summer morning was suddenly disturbed by the thundering of horse's hooves. I turned to see six horsemen dressed in Indian clothes galloping down the street toward me. My smile faltered. I didn't think they could be real Indians because we'd signed a peace treaty, but they certainly looked the part. They swooped past, slowing down beside the wagon of pioneer children. Some of the children screamed and crowded in toward the center of the wagon. One of the men grabbed a little girl about four years old and lifted her up. She began to shriek and kick as he pulled her into the saddle in front of him. He wheeled around and headed back toward my float. As they galloped past, I heard the man say in perfect English, "Don't kick my horse!" Another man in Indian costume grabbed a little boy who whooped with glee and hung onto the saddle horn, a big smile on his face. I was certainly glad the Indians hadn't decided to kidnap the Goddess of Liberty.

Toward the end of the parade, I was surprised to see Brother Yardley in the crowd. He was a middle-aged gentleman from my hometown who had never married. Because he had so far avoided the entanglements of wife and children, he was well off, dressed nattily on this holiday with polished shoes peeking out from under his pressed trousers.

"Brother Yardley!" I called, and gave him an extra vigorous wave. I saw his eyes widen in surprise before he smiled broadly and tipped his hat to me.

The parade ended much too soon. As I was helped down from my float, I noticed the little pioneer girl who had been snatched from the wagon. She was safe in the arms of a woman I assumed was her mother. The girl was clutching the lady's neck so tightly I wondered if the woman could even breathe. As I straightened my robe, I overheard the woman say, "Elizabeth, they weren't real Indians. They were just wearing costumes. It was just pretend." I glanced over at Elizabeth's face and could tell that she wasn't convinced.

Amelia didn't want to take the time to go back home for me to change out of my robe before the games started. I was secretly glad to have an excuse to wear my robe and crown a little longer, and walked around the city park with my head held high. Eventually the magical day ended and it was time to return to Amelia's house and my regular life as Frederikke.

It was several days later when I received a letter from my father. It surprised me to see his handwriting on the envelope, as my mother was the one who usually kept me updated on the family activities. I slit the envelope open and pulled out a single sheet of paper. The words I read filled me with amazement.

"Frederikke," it began, "Brother Yardley saw you in the Fourth of July parade in American Fork and was much impressed with you. He asked permission to court you, and I gave consent. He is a wealthy man who could provide a bounteous life for you. I have enclosed a return train ticket with this letter." It was signed simply, "Da."

"I don't believe it," I murmured as my hand dropped to my side, the letter dangling from my fingers.

"What's wrong, Rikky?" Amelia asked. I handed her the letter. After she read it, she looked up at me with envious eyes and said, "You are so lucky!"

I stared at her. "Why?" I asked in disbelief.

"If you marry Brother Yardley, you'll be rich," Amelia said, her face alight with the possibilities. "You could dress like a princess every day."

My heart took slight courage at the thought of any possible good from the situation, yet the obvious was staring at me in the face, so I had to protest, "But he's old!"

"How old?" Amelia demanded.

"I don't know!" I said lifting my shoulders and letting them drop again. "Thirty or forty."

"As old as your father?" Amelia asked.

I shook my head. "No, not that old. But he's pretty old."

Amelia regarded me thoughtfully. "Well, if you don't want to be rich, you could always tell your father you won't go home."

I imagined my father's stern face and his voice raised loud in disapproval. "Oh, I couldn't tell him that," I said.

"So you don't want to go and you won't tell your father you won't. What else is there?" Amelia shook her head at me as if I was a lost cause. "What could it hurt to give it a try? You might like Brother Yardley." Amelia put both of her palms up and said, "My father's fifteen years older than Mama. They get along fine."

I tried to find comfort in Amelia's words as I rode the train toward home a few days later. With each passing mile her words got fainter and fainter while my heart pounded louder and louder. By the time I met my father at the station I was so frightened at the prospect of Brother Yardley's courting that I almost told him I didn't want to do it. Before I could speak, Da smiled broadly and wrapped his arms around me. "My little Rikky, I am so proud of you." He pulled back and held me by both shoulders. "But you're not so little now, are you?" I thought I was the same as when I'd left home to work in the city six months earlier. Da brushed a strand of hair from my cheek in a gesture so tender I felt something melt inside me. I couldn't break this moment with a declaration of refusal to do his bidding.

I only had one day to move my things back into my old room and get settled when Da announced that Brother Yardley would be coming to call that afternoon. "He's taking you for a buggy ride," he told me, his face radiating satisfaction at his daughter's good fortune. I tried to smile back at him, but my mouth felt stuck. Nevertheless, I went through the motions of getting ready. It's only a buggy ride, I told myself as I pulled on the new dress that had appeared in my closet while I was gone. Mama helped me with my hair. I stared in the mirror as she brushed and twisted and pinned, seeing a stranger in the glass again. This time it was no princess, but a condemned woman who stared back at me, despair roiling deep in the depths of the wide blue eyes. It was no use. I couldn't make myself want to go riding with Brother Yardley.

"There," Mama said when she was finished. "Now you look just like a princess." She hugged me before she bustled off to the kitchen, no doubt to get some sort of fancy refreshments laid out for our visitor.

My ten-year-old brother Albert started to yell, "He's coming! He's coming!"

I heard the rush of feet toward the front of the house as my family hurried to the windows to watch my suitor's approach. Without even thinking of a plan, my feet took me out the back door. My mind blank with panic, I crawled into the first hiding place I saw that was big enough to hold me. I crouched down as small as I could make myself and hid my face in my knees. Before long, I heard my brother's and sister's voices calling, "Rikky! Rikky!" I didn't move.

The voices faded away. After several long minutes, I heard my father's voice raised in frustration. "Frederikke! Where are you?" he bellowed. I slid my hands over my ears and squeezed my eyes shut. I wasn't going to answer no matter how loud he shouted. I knew without a doubt that I'd rather face fearsome punishment from my father than to go out riding with Brother Yardley.

Da's voice abruptly stopped calling. I heard Mama's murmuring voice, but couldn't make out the words. Then I didn't hear any voices for a long time. I could see the shadows stretch slowly as the sun lowered itself toward the western horizon. My legs were getting cramped but I waited as long as I could before I dared shift my knees in an effort to find a more comfortable position. As soon as I settled into an equally cramped but slightly different posture, I heard a scuffing sound. I tensed.

A shadow moved swiftly over the opening of my hiding place. "Rikky!" Albert said in surprise. I raised my head and peered up at my little brother through the top of the empty rain barrel. "Are you stuck?" he asked.

"No," I answered sourly.

"We've been looking for you everywhere," Albert told me unnecessarily. "Brother Yardley left without you."

"Good," I said, moving my stiff legs so I could stand up.

"His buggy was wonderful," Albert said, looking off in the distance. "It was black with white fringe and brass on the wheels. I'll bet it could go as fast as a train."

"I don't care," I said, grasping the side of the rain barrel with my hands and pulling myself up onto my feet. I couldn't stifle a moan as the blood rushed back into my legs.

"I would have ridden with you," Albert said stoutly, looking up at me. Then he titled his head sideways. "I thought you liked buggy rides, Rikky."

"I do," I said, stretching the kinks out of my back. "Just not buggy rides with Brother Yardley."

"He wasn't very happy," Albert informed me solemnly. "When we couldn't find you, Mama asked him if he wanted to come in for some refreshments, and he said 'no, thank you.' Then he climbed in his buggy and rode away. He didn't even say goodbye."

I stepped over the side of the barrel, not caring if Albert saw my ankles as my new dress bunched up around my knees. He was just my little brother, and it was almost dark anyway. "Are you going in?" Albert asked me when I was standing up outside the barrel.

"Well, I'm not going to sleep outside," I announced with more courage than I felt. I marched toward the back door.

"Da's not very happy," Albert warned as I put my hand on the knob. I hesitated and glanced down at his solemn face. Well, I wasn't very happy either. I had done the only thing I could think of to stop a possible lifetime of unhappiness. I resolutely twisted the handle and stepped inside the house.

Mama looked up and saw me. "Rikky!" she said, "Are you all right?"

"She was in the rain barrel," Albert said helpfully.

"The rain barrel?" Ma said incredulously before she stole a glance at Da. Da was staring at me. I squared my shoulders and met his gaze. Da shook his head slowly before he put one hand to his mouth and looked down at his lap.

"You children had better go up to bed," Mama said quickly. I headed for the stairs, Albert right behind me. I threw one last look at my father before I disappeared through the doorway. It was hard to tell with his hand in the way, but if I'd had to guess, I would have said that my father was smiling behind his fingers.

With a light heart and Brother Yardley out of my life, I went upstairs to bed.

SHIRLEY BAHLMANN

In 1873, sixteen-year-old Frederikke (Rikky) Tollestrup was chosen to ride as Goddess of Liberty in the Fourth of July parade in American Fork. A middle-aged bachelor from her hometown of Gunnison saw the lovely Rikky and let her father, Niels, know that he was interested in courting her. When the suitor came to take Rikky riding in his new buggy, she was nowhere to be found. Eventually the would-be Romeo left, obviously displeased and put out by this shocking lack of manners. Later, Rikky's siblings found her hidden in an empty rain barrel. Her father merely looked at her in exasperation, but said no more about the courtship.

Elizabeth Jacobson Story remembers the year 1920 when as a little four-year-old she was dressed as a pioneer to ride on a horse-drawn float as part of the Fourth of July parade. One of six men dressed as Indians galloped down the parade route and snatched her from the float. As he carried her off, he admonished her not to kick his horse in her struggle to get away. When her mother finally found her, Elizabeth was so frightened she couldn't speak.

# WITH THIS RING

I looped the next stitch of royal blue yarn over my knitting needle, then took a moment to survey the length of completed sweater. I imagined how good it would look on my husband, George, after he opened it Christmas morning.

A sudden pounding on the door made me jump. I clicked my tongue in disgust when the stitch slipped off the needle. I gingerly laid my work down beside my chair. I'd try to pick up the stitch after I answered the door. As I stood, I wondered if George had heard the knock. He was in bed reading, if he hadn't fallen asleep already. As a recent medical school graduate, he often stayed in his clinic after hours and frequently made house calls at any hour. His enthusiasm for helping sick people was heartwarming, but I sometimes wondered if he was spreading himself too thin.

I pulled the door open, and gasped at what I saw. A young man who looked to be in his mid-twenties stared back at me with frenzied eyes. He leaned toward me, desperately searching my face, his hair sticking up every which way like a wild man, his cheeks pinched red with cold. "Is the doctor here?" he gasped. "Is this where he lives? Is he in?" His chapped red hands clasped together as he begged, "Please, oh, please help me."

"What's the matter?" I asked, scanning him for blood and not seeing any.

"It's my wife," he blurted.

I looked past the man but could see no one else standing with him out in the snow.

"Where is she?" I asked tersely.

"In the car," he said, his despairing eyes piercing mine. Some inner sense told me he was sincere.

"Go get her," I commanded. "Put her on the couch. I'll get Doctor Sears." I left the front door open to the freezing night and hurried to the bedroom. I found my husband with his eyes closed and his glasses sitting crookedly on his nose, a book open on his

9

lap. He was snoring softly. "George," I called, hating to wake him.

He sat up as though he'd been shocked. "What?" he said, pushing his glasses back into place. I was still amazed at how quickly he could go from sleep to full alert.

"There's someone here for you."

George threw his feet over the side of the bed. "Who is it?" he asked as he pushed his legs into his trousers.

"I don't know him," I said.

George flailed his arm at his shirt sleeve, trying to find the opening. I stepped over and helped him guide his arm into the right place. "He says his wife is sick," I said. I began to button his shirt as he fastened his trousers, but George headed for the door before I finished. I followed him out to the living room to see the disheveled young man gently lowering a young woman onto our sofa. She was hardly more than a girl, with a smooth face as pale as fine china. Even her lips were pale, like a rose faded past its full bloom. Dark hair curled across her forehead and dark eyelashes lay soft as feathers on her cheeks. She had on a blue coat of spring weight fabric, which wasn't nearly warm enough for this weather. She sank down onto the cushions without opening her eyes. I wondered if she was even alive. Her husband picked up her limp hand, and I saw a thin gold wedding band glint on her finger before he completely swallowed up her hand in both of his, as though he could keep her safe if he didn't let go.

"Let me have a look," George said. The young man moved aside reluctantly, hovering close as George put his fingers on the girl's neck, checking for a pulse. "Magda, go get my stethoscope," he said to me. As I hurried from the room, I heard him ask the man, "What's her name?"

"Mercy," the man replied unsteadily.

When I got back, George had Mercy's feet propped up on a couch cushion and an afghan tucked around her. "We need a quilt," he said to me as he took the stethoscope out of my hands. I again hurried away to get what he needed. When I came back with a puffy comforter in my arms, George told the young man to spread it over his wife.

"She needs something warm to drink. Magda, have we got some hot chocolate? Is there any soup left?"

My curiosity was powerfully strong, but I headed for the kitchen instead of wasting time asking questions. The soup we'd had for dinner was thick with vegetables bottled from my garden and chunks of beef from the butcher. I poured the leftovers in a pan on the stove and turned it on. I filled a second pan with water and put it on to boil. I gathered the powdered chocolate, canned milk and sugar I would need to mix the hot chocolate. I pulled two bowls out of the cupboard, certain that Mercy's husband could stand something warm to eat, too. I wondered how long he'd been out in the cold trying to find help for his wife. They didn't look to be very well off. I hoped there was nothing seriously wrong with her.

As I began stirring chocolate powder into the boiling water, George came into the kitchen. "How is she?" I asked, turning off the heat.

"I think she'll be all right," George said, his forehead creased with concern. "It looks like she's mainly suffering from hunger and exposure. Right now she needs rest, warmth, and nourishment. In her weakened condition she's susceptible to germs that she could normally fight off."

"Why do you look so worried?" I asked as I poured canned milk into the dark chocolate water.

"It's obvious they don't have any money," he answered. "If I send them to a hospital, they'd probably just drive out of sight of our house and spend the night in their car." George rubbed his chin ruefully. "It's not much of a car. It's an old Model T that looks to be held together with hatbox string."

"For goodness sakes, they can just stay here," I said, digging the measuring cup into the sugar bag.

George's brow smoothed out as he flashed me a smile. "I was hoping you'd think so, too!" he said. "I'm going to the infirmary to get some tonic that I think will help her. She's pretty much just worn out. When she passed out in the car, her husband thought she was dying. He was frantic."

"Yes, he was," I said dryly, tipping the sugar into the pan.

"Where do they live?"

"They're in between places right now. He's on his way to a new job in the city and has barely enough money for gas." George pushed his glasses back onto his nose as I stirred the sugar into the chocolate. "I think they're just good folks down on their luck," he said. "I'd better go get that tonic. I'll be back soon." George hurried out of the kitchen.

I carefully set a tray with filled bowls and mugs. I laid out some spoons and napkins, then carried it all into the living room. The man was kneeling beside his wife, holding her hand to his cheek. When he turned to look at me I could see tear tracks on his face. "Dinnertime!" I announced cheerfully, setting the tray on an end table. "It's nothing fancy," I apologized.

"God bless you," the man said as he picked up a bowl of soup and a spoon. He dipped the edge of the spoon into the broth, avoiding the chunks of vegetables and beef. He blew on it, touched it to his lips to check the temperature, then moved it over to his wife. "Mercy, open your mouth," he said. "Come on, darling, you need to eat," he pleaded. Without opening her eyes, Mercy's lips parted to a slit no wider than her wedding band. The man pushed the tip of the spoon into the opening and tipped it up. Mercy's throat moved as she swallowed the bit of broth. "That's my girl," her husband encouraged, a smile of relief erasing the worry lines from his forehead. He blinked rapidly several times before he could see through his tears to scoop another spoonful of soup.

"She'll be all right," I said.

"She has to be," he whispered fervently as he lifted the next spoonful to her mouth. "She's all I care about. I'd give up my job, anything, to take care of her." Mercy swallowed the next spoonful of soup and her husband rubbed the back of his hand across his forehead before he dipped the spoon into the broth again. "She deserves better than this," he said in a thick voice.

"I'll feed her," I volunteered, putting out my hand for the bowl. "You need to eat, too."

He pulled the bowl out of my reach. "After Mercy. I need to do this for her." His anguished eyes looked deeply into mine, and

I thought I could see a thread of hope in their moist depths. He turned away and lifted the spoon to his wife's mouth again as he murmured words of encouragement and praise at her efforts to eat. It seemed to me as though these two were no strangers to pitting themselves against the world. It appeared in every glance and touch that they had to turn to each other when things got hard, and they had become as much one as much as a couple could be, in spite of their youth. I felt my heart grow big with admiration for them, and hoped that the new job would be a good one. They desperately needed something good in their lives.

When George got back, Mercy had finished eating. Her bowl was only half empty, but George said it was enough. Mercy obediently swallowed the tonic George brought for her, then turned her head toward the back of the couch and relaxed into a deep sleep. George handed the bottle to the young man. "Give this to her twice a day," he said.

The man gazed longingly at the bottle but didn't reach for it. "I don't have anything to pay you with."

"It's extra," George said dismissively, stepping closer and pushing it into the man's hand. "It's nearly expired, so I'll be throwing it away next week if you don't take it now. It'd be a shame to waste it when it could be used to help your wife feel better." The young man's hand closed around the bottle.

"We've got an extra bed in the small bedroom," I said. "You could sleep there."

The man shook his head. "I'll sleep on the floor next to my wife," he declared. I knew he wouldn't be dissuaded. I left and came back with an armful of blankets and a pillow for him to use. He sat with his back against the couch and pulled a blanket over his knees before he took hold of Mercy's limp hand.

George checked Mercy's vital signs once more before he nodded in satisfaction. "Wake me at any time tonight if you're worried about anything," he said.

"Yes, I will," the man said. "Thank you." He laid his head on the couch cushion next to Mercy's body and closed his eyes.

It seemed easy for George to fall asleep. I wondered what it would be like to be able to wake up and go to sleep instantly, as easy as pulling a chain on a light. I curled up on my side and said a silent prayer in my heart for the struggling young couple in our living room before I finally drifted off to sleep.

The next morning we found Mercy sitting up, pale and disheveled, but smiling bashfully when she saw us approach. "I'm so sorry," she said softly. "I didn't mean to put everyone to so much trouble." Her husband sat beside her on the couch, one arm protectively around her shoulders and a look of absolute relief on his face.

"Are you feeling up to eating some breakfast?" I asked.

Mercy fidgeted with the edge of the comforter. "Well, yes, I am rather hungry," she admitted.

I went into the kitchen and started scrambling eggs. As I toasted thick slices of home-baked bread butter-side-down in my hot skillet, George came in. "How is she?" I asked.

"Doing quite well," George said cheerfully. "They assured me that they wanted to make payments for our services, but I told them we wouldn't accept anything. It was good enough for us to see that they were safely on their way."

"Of course," I agreed. "You did the right thing."

Mercy ate more breakfast than George, but not as much as her husband. George and I made small talk while the four of us ate. When everyone's plates were nearly empty, I excused myself and pushed away from the table. I got busy at the counter with a loaf of bread, a knife, and some cold baked ham that I was going to have for supper. Now, instead of fried ham slices, we would eat the hambone boiled in a pot of white navy beans. There was just enough ham to make four thick sandwiches. I wrapped them up in butcher paper and tied them with string.

"Here are some sandwiches for the road," I said, handing the package to Mercy.

She impulsively threw her arms around me. "Thank you," she said. "You're so kind." She pulled away and looked shyly at George. "You're kind, too," she said.

"Then where's my hug?" George asked, a bereft look on his face. Mercy giggled and gave him a quick squeeze.

Her husband took my hand and shook it with both of his. "God bless you," he said, letting go and extending his hand to George. "God bless both of you," he said fervently.

We waved to the couple from our front door as they rattled off in their old car. The excessive exhaust from the car quickly obscured the old black rattletrap. We could hear it even after we couldn't see it anymore.

"I need to get ready for work," George told me as he turned toward the bathroom.

"All right. I'll just tidy up," I said. I skirted around the blue sweater on the floor, the slipped stitch forgotten in last night's drama. I headed for the couch and folded up the comforter, then spread the afghan over the backrest. I pulled up the pillow and began to tug the pillowslip off when I noticed a piece of crumpled paper where the pillow had been. I bent over and picked it up, then carefully unfolded it. As I pulled back the paper from the last fold, my eyes widened in surprise. A thin, plain gold wedding band lay in the middle of the scrawled note. We can't pay, but we don't want to owe. Take this ring and our deepest thanks.

"George!" I called as I hurried toward the bathroom door.

He stuck his head out of the doorway, half of his jaw covered with white lather. "What is it?" he asked.

"Look!" I said, handing him the note and the ring. He picked up the ring with two fingers and read the note. He shook his head sadly. "They didn't need to do that," he said. "But I understand why they did."

"Did you ever get their last name?" I asked.

"No. I never asked, and they never said."

"Where was he going to work?"

George turned his eyes toward the ceiling for a few moments before he lowered his gaze to look at me. "I don't know that he ever said," he answered as he handed the ring and the note back to me.

The ring felt heavy in my hand. "Maybe they'll come back for it," I said. "Perhaps they only meant for us to keep it until they

15

earned some money to pay us, then they'll be back to claim it."

George's eyes lit up. "That could be," he said. "They do know where we live. It would be easy for them to get in touch with us."

"I'll put this in a safe place," I said, my heart light with the hope of someday returning the ring. I made my way to the bedroom where I found a small box that George's Christmas cufflinks had come in. I nestled the ring into the small square of cushiony cotton at the bottom. I folded up the note small enough to tuck in on top of the ring, and closed the lid.

Over the years, I periodically came across the little box with its sad treasure. I would open it, re-read the note, and wonder what had become of Mercy and her husband. They never came back for the ring.


*In the early 1900's, Doctor George Sears was roused one night by a desperate young man who was traveling through town with his wife. Dr. Sears and his wife Magnola took care of the sick young woman in their own home. The next morning they forgave the young couple any debt and sent them on their way. When they cleaned up after the evening's events, they found the young woman's wedding ring wrapped in a note of thanks for their kindness and help. Although it was kept safe in a drawer, the young couple never returned for it. Magnola showed the ring to her daughter, Lois Sears Brown, who re-told the story.*

# GIFT OF GAB

I elbowed Wally out of the way and scrambled up the train steps ahead of him, grabbing the railing at the top to catch my balance when my snow-slick shoes threatened to send me skating down the aisle. As I stopped to shake snow from my pant cuffs and stomp my shoes free of the icy stuff, Wally jostled me from behind. "Get a move on, Sherman, some of us want to get warm."

"Hold your horses," I shot back. "Some of us want to keep from falling on our fannies." I gave Wally a backward butt before I started down the aisle to find a seat. Then I saw her watching me. The girl couldn't have been more than twenty, with soft waves of chestnut brown hair that curled alluringly around her ears. Her lovely figure was clothed in a burgundy dress. Large brown eyes regarded me curiously as her full, pink mouth curved with the hint of a smile. I wondered with a hot flash of sudden embarrassment if she had heard what I'd said to Wally. I hoped not.

My heart fluttered in alarm when I saw that the seat opposite the beautiful young lady was empty. I didn't dare take it. I could smooth talk the hometown girls who were my own age, which was eighteen, but this was completely different. I knew that if I tried to converse with this pretty stranger, my tongue would trip all over itself.

I abruptly turned and slid into a seat that was across the aisle but just ahead of where the girl was sitting. From my vantage point, I could watch her without being blatant. Wally plopped down onto the seat opposite me. Each pair of seats on the train faced one another so that four people could sit and converse comfortably as they rode to their destinations.

"Boy, Sherm, I never thought when Christmas break started that I'd be looking forward to school again," Wally said as he stretched his legs out long in front of him.

"Yeah, me too," I said absently, my eyes glued to the girl. She was casually watching other people find seats along the train car. She had an open and friendly expression. Maybe I could speak to her after all. But what would I say? If I could only think of an impressive opening line, there was still time to change my seat. Wally could even tag along. Maybe he would sit beside me like a gentleman instead of sprawling all over his seat like a scarecrow missing some stuffing. Maybe not. If I took Wally, he'd probably make a mess of things. I'd be better off to go alone. But Wally would follow me anyway, asking me where I was going and why I was changing seats. There was nothing sophisticated about Wally.

"Sherman? What are you staring at?" Wally said, craning his neck around to look behind him. The girl noticed his movements and fastened her deep brown eyes on me.

"Turn around!" I hissed at Wally through my teeth as I quickly dropped my eyes.

"She's a looker," Wally said as he turned back to face me. I stared hard at him. "What's with you, Sherm?" Wally's eyebrows raised along with his question. Then a wicked little smile turned up the corners of his mouth. "Oh, Sherman, are you in love?" he taunted.

"Shut up," I said. "How can I be in love with someone I don't even know?"

Wally extended his hand into the aisle. "Go introduce yourself," he said too loudly. "Your carriage seat is empty, Prince Charming."

"Your head is empty," I growled at him before I folded my arms stubbornly across my chest.

I felt a hard bump against my shoulder and shot a look up into a man's square jawed face. He sported a pencil thin moustache on his upper lip. "Oh, sorry," he said as he pulled his sales case closer in to his body. He smiled with perfect teeth and nodded his head in apology, his smart-looking bowler hat bobbing agreeably. As soon as he finished speaking to me and turned his head forward, I knew he'd seen her. I could tell because his shoulders pulled up straighter, his head tipped, and there was a slight pause before he stepped forward.

"Is this seat taken?" he asked the pretty girl in a deep voice as smooth as butter.

"No," she answered. An adorable little smile played around her mouth.

My heart swelled with a curious mix of pain from missed opportunity and relief from removal of temptation. I reasoned that I couldn't very well sit across from her if there was already someone else there. The salesman set his case on the floor and leaned back into his seat. He removed his hat and expertly pulled a hand over his hair to smooth it into place. "Trains are one of the best inventions ever," he said as he laid one arm casually along the back of his seat. "Imagine having to make this trip in an open air wagon."

The girl's face drew up in sudden consternation. "That would be so cold!" she said, sliding her hands around her elbows.

The salesman's voice continued confidently. "Fortunately, you don't have to worry about a thing. You'll ride warm, safe and sound until you need to get off at...?" He paused to let her fill in the blank. He acted as though he was the man to personally thank for the young woman's journey being a pleasant one.

"Did you hear that?" I whispered to Wally. The train floor rumbled under my feet as we pulled out of the station.

"What?" Wally asked, rummaging in his valise for a packet of sandwiches that his mother had tucked somewhere inside.

"He found out where her stop is."

"So? I could have done that," Wally pulled the linen napkin back from the double stack of bread in his hand. "Just ask her."

"No, no, that's too bold. You put girls off if you're too bold."

Wally's forehead creased in puzzlement as he bit into the sandwich. He didn't even bother to swallow before he asked, "What about brave, bold and daring? Aren't those things a girl wants in a man?"

"That's different," I said impatiently. "Listen, Wally, we could learn some things from this guy. He's suave."

Wally shrugged. "My mother taught me that listening to other people's conversations is eavesdropping." Wally swallowed his bite of sandwich before he said, "Not that I mind eavesdropping on occasion, but it has to be something interesting before I stoop so low." He lowered his head and looked up at me, making his eyebrows a stern barrier as a schoolmaster might while scolding a cheating pupil.

19

I gripped my armrest and leaned forward. "This is education-al," I said firmly. "If we learn some of his methods, we'll be able to talk to girls when we get back to school."

"I can talk just fine," Wally said. "Any girl that doesn't like the way I talk isn't worth talking to." He took another bite of his sand-wich. "Want some?" he asked through his unchewed mouthful as he extended the sandwich toward me.

"No, you eat it," I said, exasperated. He did. After he'd swal-lowed the last bite, he leaned his head back and went to sleep, his mouth falling open like a fish going after bait. I was glad for the absence of his opinion until he started to snore. The noise made it hard to eavesdrop on my unwary tutor.

After a while, we pulled to a stop in Thistle Junction. The conductor announced that we were awaiting a connecting train from Price before we continued our journey. His announcement woke up Wally, who yawned hugely, stretched his arms high over-head and announced, "I've got to go answer nature's call. What about you, Sherm?"

"Oh, keep your voice down, will ya?" I said in a hoarse whis-per. Several people got up to stretch their legs and wander about the small train station, including Wally and me. After we took care of necessities and worked out some kinks, we got settled in our seats again. I noticed the salesman walking with the girl as they made their way back to their places. I could hear her giggling and wished I knew what the salesman had said to her. I re-dedicated myself to learn as much as I could from this man while I had the opportunity. As the couple sat down opposite each other, I leaned forward and slightly out into the aisle with my elbow on my knee and my chin on my hand. I hoped I looked casual.

"Hey, Sherm, what are you ..." Wally began.

I was just getting ready to tell him to mind his own business and do something useful like stare out the window when a sudden jolt threw me off my seat and into the empty spot beside Wally. My eyes were wide with surprise as I caught the back of the seat with my hands. I had a perfect view of the salesman in the same predicament I was in. He had also been thrown forward, but since he had placed himself directly opposite the girl, he was in danger of bumping heads with her. He threw his hands out at the last second, bracing them on either side of her head. Something flew out of his mouth and landed in the girl's lap as he took the sudden weight of his body on his extended arms. My face reddened in sympathetic embarrassment for him. Pushing himself quickly away from the back of the seat, the salesman boldly snatched whatever it was from the girl's lap. Her expression of shock made me mighty curious. A partially chewed bite of bread would more likely elicit a feeling of disgust. I should know. I threw a withering glance at Wally.

"Whoa, what was that?" Wally asked, looking out the window.

I looked back at the salesman in time to see him whirl away from the girl and stalk down the aisle, his mouth pressed together in a mushy line. I glanced down at his hand and glimpsed a set of false teeth peering out from between his fingers. Little wonder there was no smile on his face. It was clutched in his hand. The salesman disappeared out the door at the end of the train, which led to the next car.

"Well, look at that," Wally said in delight as he pointed a finger at the window. "The Price train must have bad brakes. It bumped right into us!"

After the new cars were coupled to our train, we again got underway. The salesman never returned to his seat. Even when we pulled into the Salt Lake City train station there was no sign of the girl's missing seatmate. She stood and brushed her skirt absently with a gloved hand before she made her way down the aisle and off the train. It was then that I noticed the salesman's case sitting crookedly between the two facing seats.

"Wally! Look at that!" I said, pointing. "Do you think we should take it?"

"Oh, eavesdropping isn't enough for you. Now you want to become a thief, too," Wally chastised me.

"I didn't mean it like that," I answered defensively. "What if the salesman was so embarrassed that he got off the train at Thistle and left his case behind? How's he going to know where to find it?"

"How would you know where to find him?" Wally asked reasonably. "Look, Sherm, the D&RGW deal with lost luggage all the time. They'll know what to do with it. Come on, let's get going."

Wally led the way. I kept hanging back, feeling for some reason that I had to keep my eye on the case. Wally finally managed to pull me off the train and onto the ground. "Quit dragging your feet," he complained. "We're the last ones off the train."

As I followed my friend toward the station exit, I threw one more look back over my shoulder. Framed in the doorway of the train car was the salesman. He stood on the bottom step, his head turning right, then left, then right again. Seeming to satisfy himself with what he saw, or maybe what he didn't see, he quickly stepped down and hurried away, his teeth clamped firmly in his jaws, and his sales case gripped tightly in his hand.

*In the early 1900's, Sherman H. Reusch tells of the time he was riding the D&RGW (Denver and Rio Grande Western) train with his boarding school mate Wallace Wintch. They were impressed by a salesman or "drummer" who was engaging a pretty young lady in conversation. The boys were awed with his suave talk until a locomotive from an adjoining spur misjudged the distance and bumped into the back of their train. The resulting jolt caused the salesman to fall forward, his mouth open in amazement, his false teeth jarred out of his mouth and onto the girl's lap as he strove to keep from bumping heads with her. The salesman bolted from the car, teeth in hand, and didn't return for his sales case until everyone was off the train.*

# TROLL PRINCE

The clouds on the horizon were thin and gray, hanging limply in the air. I glanced over at the sailcloth tent that I had called home ever since the train left us at the end of the line in Florence, Nebraska. I knew that sailcloth worked to propel ships across the ocean, but would it keep out the rain?

Hanna Nelson pushed her head out from the tent flap. We had been assigned to the same tent since she was also single and about my same age of twenty-two. Hanna's dark hair was mussy around her pale, oval face. Her ocean blue eyes turned toward the horizon. As pretty as she was, she wasn't very industrious, so my opinion of her was less than it might have been. Her hands were slender and soft while my own square hands were chapped and work-roughened. From the time I was a little girl in Sweden, I had learned to keep myself busy, and I was impatient with idleness. Nevertheless, Hanna was good company while we waited for a wagon escort to meet us and take us the rest of the way to Salt Lake City.

"Wagons?" Hanna asked.

I whipped my head toward the horizon. I noticed small, humped shapes moving slowly along beneath the haze that I now recognized as dust clouds. I had to shade my eyes against the evening sun before I could identify the shapes as covered wagons. "Wagons!" I yelled, excited at the prospect of resuming our journey at last.

Several people gathered at the edge of camp to see the wagons for themselves. Hanna stood and walked over to my side. We all cheered as the wagons pulled into a circle beside our little tent colony. Some of the men were waving their hats. I quickly pulled the red scarf off my head that I sometimes used to keep my light brown hair out of my face and swung it joyously through the air.

A tall man wearing a beard streaked with gray drove the lead wagon. He pulled his team of mules to a stop and climbed down. Our company leader met him with a fervent handshake. The other wagon drivers climbed down from their seats. Some made a beeline for the bushes while others extended their hands and called cheerful greetings to us. One man began to hug the Saunders family all around. I guessed he was related to them.

Sixteen-year-old Johanna Anderson wandered over to stand close to the youngest teamster. He looked to be somewhere in his twenties. He had a firm jaw and a back as straight as a ship's mast. He kept throwing appreciative glances at Johanna. I shook my head at her lack of propriety. She was such a flirt.

The gray-bearded man held up his hands. "Brothers and sisters," he called. Most of us quieted down to listen. "I am your wagon master, Brother Standing. I will be dividing your company among the wagons. Load your belongings under the supervision of your teamster. If he says you have too much, you must pare down to his satisfaction. Only those who become ill or infirm will ride."

Brother Standing paused while the air filled with moans and exclamations of surprise. I saw old Sister Belnap hunch herself over a little more and put a few more wrinkles in her brow with a worried frown. When the outburst quieted down, Brother Standing continued. "Most of you will travel on foot in order to spare the oxen. If you have any questions, ask your teamster. We will depart three days from now so the animals can rest."

Brother Standing looked down at a paper in his hand. "Brother Daniel Clegg," he called. The youngest teamster lifted his hand and nodded to Brother Standing as he touched the brim of his hat. Johanna remained standing nearby. "You will take Peter and Johanna Anderson and the Blakelock family in your wagon." I saw Johanna turn a pleased shade of pink when she heard that she and her older brother Peter would be traveling with the handsome young wagon driver. Teamster Clegg gave her a nod and a grin before he moved around his wagon to unhitch his team.

Brother Standing made a few more assignments before he called, "Brother Hakan Anderson." A man with merry eyes and thinning brown hair stepped forward. His shoulders were sloped as though he had worked too hard as a youth. Although he wasn't as old as Brother Standing, he was as bent as a tree growing up in too many windstorms. If he hadn't been stoop shouldered, he would have been taller than Brother Standing. Both men had beards, but Brother Standing's was full and included a moustache. Brother

Anderson's was a simple fringe of hair around his jawline. "You will take Sister Cecelia Swenson, Sister Hanna Nelson, and Sister Margaret Belnap. Will you sisters please raise your hands?" I quietly envied Johanna her handsome young man as I raised my hand.

Brother Anderson moved toward us with a delighted smile on his face. "It looks like I'm destined to be surrounded by beautiful women," he said. Hanna giggled. Sister Belnap put her hand up to her wrinkled mouth as she looked coquettishly out of the corners of her eyes at our teamster.

"Ha," I said.

Brother Anderson's eyes found mine. "You don't think you're beautiful?" he asked.

I wasn't sure how to answer that. I wasn't used to such direct questions. I knew that my light brown hair did not even compare to Hanna's dark mane, and my blue eyes paled next to hers. My face was round and my shoulders were broad. "No," I said finally.

"Then maybe I'll have to convince you," Brother Anderson said gently. My heart fluttered as I stared into his soft blue eyes, which sported generous smile crinkles at their corners.

"You can call me Hanna," Hanna said, breaking the spell that locked my eyes to Brother Anderson's.

"Call me Hakan," he told her with a little bow.

"I'm Sissla," I said quickly.

"Sissla," Hakan said slowly. "That's pretty."

"And you can call me Sister Belnap," Sister Belnap said, her hands folded primly on the front of her skirt.

"Pleased to meet you, Sister Belnap," Hakan said as he took her hand and bent over it in a courtly gesture.

That night after supper, Hanna offered to go with Hakan to check on his team. I watched them disappear around the back of the wagon with my hands on my hips. I couldn't remember the last time Hanna had offered to help with anything. Usually I had to ask her to help me.

A little five-year-old orphan girl named Aggie walked up

behind me and tugged on my skirt. "Sissla," she said, "Will you tell me a story?"

I glanced down at the little girl who had watched both of her parents slide into watery graves during our sea voyage. She had been assigned to the Blakelock family's care until we reached Zion, but I didn't think the Blakelocks were used to having her in their family circle yet. Aggie often wandered the camp, looking for scraps of attention wherever she could find them.

"All right," I agreed. I led Aggie back to a stool by my tent and sat down. Pulling her onto my lap, I began, "Once upon a time there was a troll."

"Was he the troll that hid under the bridge so he could jump out to eat the three billy goats gruff?" Aggie asked solemnly.

"That must have been a Norwegian troll," I said. "I'm talking about Swedish trolls, who live in the woods and are curious and gentle."

"I thought trolls were bad," Aggie said.

"No, not bad." I shifted in my seat as I sought a way to explain my country's folklore. "Sometimes they're mischievous, but that's because they want to make friends with humans and don't know how. Trolls might curdle your milk or hide your shoes or even switch their infants for human babies. That's because they think humans are so beautiful.

"Are trolls ugly?" Aggie asked me.

"That depends on what you think is ugly," I said. "Unless they're an underground troll, they're usually big. They have large hands and feet, but move quietly in the forest where they talk to moose and bears. Sometimes they're stoop shouldered which makes their arms look longer, and the men might wear a fringe of beard."

"Like Brother Anderson?" Aggie asked.

I stopped and thought for a moment, and then I smiled. "Yes, perhaps a little like Brother Anderson."

With several more interruptions from Aggie, I finally finished the story and walked her back to the Blakelock's wagon. Sister

Blakelock absently took her by the hand and tucked her in beside her own little girl. I made my way back to my tent and ducked inside to find Hanna already there, crawling around on her hands and knees as she straightened her blankets. She turned and sat down when she heard me come in. "Guess what, Sissla? Hakan's not married," she said smugly.

"So what?" I shrugged. "He's a widower."

"He's never been married." Hanna wrapped her arms around her knees.

I looked at Hanna. "Is something wrong with him?" I asked. "He's pretty old not to be married."

"He's only thirty-seven," Hanna said defensively. "He's kind of shy."

"Ha!" I exclaimed. "He didn't seem a bit shy when he said we were all beautiful!"

Hanna waved her hand. "That's just bluster. You don't know him like I do."

"One evening with the oxen and you're best friends?" I asked incredulously.

"He's so sweet!" Hanna insisted. She rested an elbow on her knee and lowered her chin onto her hand. "I think it's so romantic that he hasn't found the right girl in thirty-seven years. He's like a knight on a quest."

"Aggie thinks he looks like a troll," I said.

Hanna sat up indignantly. "Looks aren't everything."

"Johanna seems to think a lot of that handsome Brother Clegg," I said, enjoying Hanna's distress in some perverse corner of my heart.

Hanna sputtered for a moment before she found the words she wanted to say. "Is he good? Is he kind? That's what matters, not your hair or face or the bend of your back." I was too tired to think of anything to say in reply, so I tucked myself into bed and went to sleep.

The next couple of days ran together in busy preparation for the trek to Zion. On the day before we were to leave, I noticed Johanna and Daniel at their wagon. They each had hold of opposite handles on her trunk as they swung it up into the wagon bed. Johanna undid the clasp and lifted out a bright red coat. "My mother made it for me," she told Daniel as she fingered the fabric. "The last time I ever had it on was for Mama to sew up the hem. The next day Peter and I got on the boat." She smoothed an imaginary wrinkle from the coat. "Sometimes when I miss my mother it helps to take it out and hold it." Johanna looked up shyly at the young man by her side. "I guess that sounds silly to you."

"Well, no, I sure can understand that," Daniel said, scratching the back of his neck. "But I know if you ever wear that coat on the trail, it'll be like dead buffalo stench pulling in coyotes."

I stopped in my tracks at his words. Johanna stared at him as though he'd grown fangs. Her eyes narrowed before she spat out hotly, "Are you insulting me or my mother?"

Daniel put his hands up defensively. "Neither," he said. "It's just that Indians are attracted to things brightly colored or shiny. They're kind of like human pack rats." Daniel gestured at the fabric clutched in Johanna's hands. "If you wear that it will be like saying 'come and get me!' I'm just telling you I wouldn't wear it if I were you. Coyotes can't help coming to carrion, and Indians can't help taking whatever they want."

Johanna was shaking her head before Daniel had even stopped talking. "I won't wear it," she said. "I'm saving it for when we get to Zion." I saw Daniel nod his head in approval as Johanna carefully folded her coat back into her trunk.

That night after prayers, Hanna said she was tired and crawled into the tent without even trying to follow Hakan for his nightly check of the stock animals. The anticipation of tomorrow's departure must have worn her out. It had the opposite effect on me. I didn't feel a bit sleepy. I wandered restlessly in the dusky light that wrapped itself around our campsite just after sunset. I made sure everything that could possibly be packed was secured inside the wagon.

Just as I was thinking I should turn in, I heard a little voice that sounded a lot like Aggie, but I couldn't make out what she was saying. She must have strayed from the Blakelock's again. I started around the corner of the wagon with a reprimand on my lips. Aggie shouldn't be wandering off when we were on the eve of our journey into the wilderness. If she didn't break her roaming habit, she could get lost. When I cleared the corner of the wagon, I was brought up short by what I saw. A dark silhouette was bending over a smaller shape that was pressed up against the side of the wagon. "Aggie?" I called, my heart thumping in alarm.

Aggie ducked away from the shape looming over her and ran to me, her arms held out beseechingly. I snatched her up into the safety of my embrace before I recognized the larger shape. It was Hakan. He straightened up as much as he was able. "It's broken!" Aggie wailed.

"What did he break?" I asked gently.

"No, you did it!" Aggie accused me. "You broke my cradle!"

"What cradle?" I asked, thoroughly confused.

"It's a kerchief cradle," Hakan said as he walked over to us. "Here, sweetheart, I'll fix it for you." Hakan pulled a crumpled white handkerchief from Aggie's hands and shook it out smooth with a single snap of his wrist. The white fabric showed plainly in the dusky light of the fading day, making it possible for me to follow his movements as Hakan folded the cloth diagonally from corner to corner into a triangle. He rolled the points in toward each other along the fold until they met in the middle in the form of two rolls of fabric. Then he pulled the back piece of fabric under the twin rolls as he held the top piece steady in place. "There you go," he said to Aggie, who carefully took the handkerchief by the corners and swung it back and forth. I supposed the rolls of fabric in the center of the "cradle" were supposed to be babies, but either they didn't have heads or they were completely covered up by their blankets. "Now you can take your babies to bed with you," Hakan said.

"Thank you Brother Troll," Aggie said, leaning over and giving Hakan a kiss on the cheek. "I love you."

Hakan scratched his head in bewilderment. "I hope that means I'm a good troll," he said uncertainly.

"Oh, yes!" Aggie assured him. "Sissla told me about good trolls like you."

"Away we go, it's past your bedtime," I said as I hurried Aggie toward the Blakelock's campsite. I imagined I could feel Hakan's eyes burning into my back at the same time my face was burning red.

I was up the next morning when it was barely light. I hurried breakfast and helped to load our tent and bedrolls. Hakan climbed up onto the wagon seat and clicked his tongue at the ox team as he flicked the reins over their backs. I was glad to begin walking, glad for the exercise after days of waiting. Around mid-day I noticed Sister Belnap lagging behind as she struggled to keep up with us. Hanna was drooping as she stepped along behind me, her eyes fixed to my shoes. As the sun sank toward the horizon, so did my enthusiasm. I had thought the train ride to Nebraska was bad, with all those little graybacks in the cushioned velvet seats biting me until I wanted to scream. It made me think of sin, the way those seats were so inviting and soft, but once you got settled in, the insects about ate you alive, like the devil would do if you ever got comfortable in sinful ways. Now there were no velvet cushions, but my own two feet feeling every stone under the thin soles of my worn down shoes.

When we circled for evening camp, Sister Belnap sunk down into the dirt right where she stood. Hakan jumped down and knelt beside her, his brow furrowed with concern. "Are you all right?" He asked.

"I can't go any more," she said, tears running streaks through the dust on her wrinkled face.

"My legs are tired, too," Hanna said petulantly.

Hakan looked up at me with helpless eyes. "Come on," I said as I limped over and took Sister Belnap's arm. "You can rest on your bedroll while we set up the tent. You'll be all right."

As soon as I took Sister Belnap off his hands, Hanna claimed Hakan's attention. "My feet hurt!" she said.

"You can rest now," Hakan soothed her. "We're camping here tonight. Brother Standing stopped the wagons earlier than usual so you can gradually get used to walking."

"You mean I have to walk further tomorrow?" Hanna asked, her eyes wide with distress. "I can't do it," she declared. "I just can't."

Hakan murmured something I couldn't hear as Hanna leaned into his shoulder. I got Sister Belnap settled and gathered up the cooking utensils. Hakan had somehow talked Hanna into helping him unload the tent. Perhaps he told her that the sooner the tent was up, the sooner she could rest.

The tent fell to the ground in a dirty white lump. Hakan looked over at me, weariness etched in the lines around his eyes. "I need to unhitch the team," he said. "Do you think you and Hanna can get this set up?"

Hanna threw a startled glance at Hakan. "I need to gather wood for cooking," she said. "I'm sure we're all famished."

Hakan bent over, grabbed the sailcloth, and began to pull the tent away from the wagon. "I can do it," I said stoutly as I grabbed a corner of the tent and pulled along with him for a couple of steps. "You go see to the animals."

Hakan gave me a grin that transformed his tired face. "You're beautiful," he said just before he turned to go. Pleasure from his praise bloomed unexpectedly in my heart.

Hanna was standing directly in Hakan's path. "I'll go with you," she said eagerly. "First I'll help you with the animals, then you can help me find wood." My pleasure melted into a puddle of disappointment as I turned back to my lonely task.

After eating, it was time for group meeting and prayer. Sister Belnap refused to go with us until Hakan threatened to carry her if necessary. He circled one arm around her old shoulders and kept pace with her, never seeming impatient or sorry that he had been the one saddled with an old lady and two young women who could barely even walk.

The gathering was a somber one until Brother Standing stood in the center of the circle and praised the company for the progress we'd made. There was not another group of saints who'd traveled farther than we had on their first day out. Our spirits lifted as we absorbed his encouraging words. When the fiddler struck up a lively tune, I felt my feet moving to the catchy rhythm. Several of the younger members of our company stood up and began a Virginia Reel. Hakan pulled Hanna out into the group as she laughingly protested. "Shy my eye," I grumbled to myself as I folded my arms into a barrier across my chest.

A little while later, Hakan singled me out and coaxed me for a dance. It was funny how my feet didn't feel as tired as they had when I was setting up the tent by myself. Maybe eating supper had given me strength. Maybe it was Hakan, who danced with amazing energy and an unstoppable smile.

After my turn, Hakan took Sister Belnap by the hand and turned her in a couple of slow circles while she tittered like a schoolgirl. I noticed one of the men who had been assigned guard duty hurry over to Brother Standing and speak earnestly into his ear. Brother Standing looked at the man sharply, then hurried after him through a gap between two of the wagons that formed a broken circle of canvas wall around us. Daniel Clegg and Peter Anderson stood up and hurried after the two men. Peter cast an anxious glance back toward the campfire before his face faded into the darkness and I could no longer read his expression .

I wondered what was wrong. Perhaps some wild animal had ventured too close and was threatening the livestock. Maybe an ox or mule was injured. I'd heard of milk cows being yoked to wagons in times of emergency when no other animals were available.

A little while later, Hakan was swinging little Aggie around in a dance loosely resembling a quadrille when I saw Brother Standing, Daniel, and Peter return quietly to the fireside. Johanna turned her head toward her brother and said something. Peter shook his head and moved his mouth in reply, but I couldn't hear what he said. When Peter pulled Johanna out to the center of the circle for a dance, she smiled at him and I supposed that whatever the problem had been, it was now taken care of.

When Brother Standing stopped the fiddler and called out to the company that it was time to turn in, I found myself walking with Sister Belnap while Hanna claimed the spot at Hakan's side. I circled Sister Belnap's shoulders with my arm as I'd seen Hakan do in order to lend her support. I tried to ignore the murmuring of voices I heard behind me as Hakan and Hanna spoke softly to each other. What did I care? I wasn't attracted to trolls. Not even nice ones.

The next morning I was surprised when Hakan helped Sister Belnap up into the wagon driver's seat. She arranged her skirts around her as though she was sitting on a throne, and eagerly set her face toward the west. I leaned over to Hanna. "Sister Belnap isn't driving the team, is she?" I whispered.

"No," Hanna answered. "Look." She pointed to the oxen. "It looks like Hakan is going to walk." Hakan held the reins in his hand as he stood beside the ox team. He clicked his tongue and slapped the reins. The ox closest to Hakan swung his thick horns around to the side, giving the teamster a curious glance. The animal's yoke mate took a step forward, bringing the ox's attention back to the task of pulling the wagon westward.

By mid-day, Sister Belnap's face was pinched with distress as she held on to the wagon seat with both hands. She called to Hakan who whoad the oxen, then walked over to look up at her with genuine concern. "Get me down," she said.

"What's wrong?" Hakan asked reaching up to support her as she climbed to the ground.

"This wagon rattles my bones something awful," she said. "Instead of sore feet, now I'm sore all over. I think I'll walk for awhile."

After Brother Standing called a stop for evening camp, Hakan followed the wagons ahead of him into the usual circle. It was then that I noticed riders approaching from the west. When I shaded my eyes to see them better, fear stirred in the pit of my stomach. Indians. I jumped when Hanna suddenly gripped my arm. She'd seen them, too. The one in the lead appeared to have red war paint splashed over his shoulders and chest. "God help us," Sister Belnap whispered as she tottered toward us.

The three of us huddled next to the wagon, gripping each other's hands as we watched the Indians approach. Brother Standing walked out toward the horsemen so that he would be the first one they met. I could see now that the red shoulders weren't painted. They were covered with some sort of cape, which flapped up and down behind the Indian as he proudly rode his horse to the edge of camp. When he slid down to greet Brother Standing, I felt a shock of surprise when I realized the Indian was wearing a red coat with the arms tied across his chest. I'd seen that coat before in Johanna's trunk. How had the Indian gotten it?

I searched the faces of the frightened travelers until I found Johanna staring at the Indian in disbelief. She broke away from the group and ran to the back of the wagon where her trunk sat. She flung open the lid. "No!" she gasped before she covered her face with her hands and began to cry. Peter hurried over and put his arm around his sister's heaving shoulders. She stiffened and pulled away from him. The Indians were given flour, sugar, and jerked beef before they left. The red coat flapped a final good-bye as the Indians rode over a rise and disappeared.

Peter was beseeching Johanna as she stalked past our wagon. "I had to," he pled. "They threatened to attack. Your coat was the only thing I could think of when Daniel Clegg said that something brightly colored or shiny would pacify them."

"Mother made it for me!" Johanna yelled at him.

"She'd rather have you alive than have the coat," Peter said before they moved out of earshot.

Johanna wasn't at the campfire that night. Peter sat at the edge of the group, his long face a sorry sight to behold. Before I could change my mind, I suddenly slid away from my place by the fire. I found Johanna curled up on a blanket underneath her wagon, her face buried in the crook of her arm. At first I thought she was asleep, but she flung her head up defensively as I approached. "Go away," she snapped. Then she lowered her eyes. "Sorry, Sissla. I thought you were Peter."

I lowered myself to the ground and leaned against a wagon wheel. "I can see how it would hurt to lose that beautiful coat," I said.

"How can anyone know how it feels?" Johanna answered bitterly. "My mother made it just for me. I was saving it for Zion."

"I can tell that your mother loves you very much. So much that she was inspired," I said.

Johanna's eyes grew large. "Inspired how?" she asked.

"If she hadn't finished the coat before you left, what could Peter have given to the Indians? Your mother may have thought she was making the coat to protect you from the cold, but it served a greater purpose than that. It protected your life."

Johanna was silent for a few moments before she said, "I never thought of it like that."

"Your mother would be very proud of Peter for looking after you as well as he has," I said. "It took a lot of courage for him to give that coat away when he knew how much it meant to you. He loves you a lot."

"Yes," Johanna said, a catch in her voice cutting the word off short. After a few minutes, she said thickly, "I still miss my mother." I reached in under the wagon and covered Johanna's hand with mine while she cried. I didn't know what else to say to comfort her. Then I thought of something. I pulled my hand away and untied my headscarf. I shook it out and folded it as I had seen Hakan do. I rolled in the sides of the triangle and pulled the bottom piece of fabric underneath the rolls as I held the top piece in place. I was proud of my accomplishment as I gazed down at the two headless babies in the fabric cradle.

"Johanna?" I said hesitantly. She wiped her eyes and looked at me, her misery stamped plain on her face. I hesitated. Johanna was several years older than Aggie. She'd probably think the babies in the cradle were stupid. I was sorry I had even thought of it.

Johanna looked at my hands. "What's that?" she asked as she crawled out from between the wheels to see better.

"It's supposed to be a little cradle," I said. "Those bundles in the middle are the babies." I nervously began to swing the fabric back and forth, rocking the cradle as the two fabric rolls snuggled together in the center.

Johanna's face brightened. "May I try?" she asked as she held out her hands. I gladly handed her the corners of the cradle and she swung the babies back and forth, back and forth, seeming to take comfort from the rhythm of the gentle movement. "That's so sweet," she said.

"Keep it," I said.

Johanna looked up at me hopefully. "May I?"

"Yes."

"Will you show me how to make it?" she asked. With a light heart, I shook out the scarf, then let Johanna watch as I rolled it into the baby cradle. She took it from me, shook it out, and made one herself. "Thank you," she said, impulsively throwing her arms around me.

I saw Hakan walking toward us. "There you are!" he said. "To what lengths will you go to avoid dancing with me? And Miss Anderson! Would you do me the honor of one dance?"

"Yes, thank you," Johanna said. She stood and moved to the back of the wagon where she opened her trunk and laid the baby cradle inside. She shut the lid. "Don't either of you dare tell Peter that's in there," she admonished us sternly before we made our way back to the bonfire.

There were many more days of walking before we finally descended into the Salt Lake Valley. I was overjoyed to see the houses and other signs of civilization. Sister Belnap met her two sons who took her home with them. Aggie found her aunt and uncle. Johanna had made up with Peter, and they went to live with relatives. Other families in our wagon train were assigned building lots. I didn't know a soul in Salt Lake City, and I wondered what would become of me.

"Hanna, what are you going to do now?" I asked.

"I don't know," she said. "I suppose I might see if I can find work."

"Doing what?" I asked.

Hanna shrugged and turned helpless eyes to me. Then she smiled ruefully. "I could feed livestock," she said.

I couldn't help but laugh. "Whatever we do, we'll do it together," I announced as I linked my arm in hers.

Hanna gave me a genuine smile and said fervently, "Really?" She hugged my arm to her side. "I feel safe with you, Sissla."

A voice sounded from behind us. "What? No one to meet you two beautiful ladies?" We turned to see Hakan standing stoop-shouldered beside his team and wagon as he surveyed us both with his merry blue eyes.

"We don't know anyone here," Hanna confessed.

"Perhaps you'd like to come with me, then," he said. "I live in a small settlement called Pleasant Creek. It's not as big as Salt

Lake City, but it's pretty." I wouldn't hesitate to put myself in Hakan's care. I grinned as I recalled Aggie calling him a good troll. He was the prince of trolls.

"Yes, please," Hanna said, answering for both of us.

It took us five days to get to Pleasant Creek. Hakan introduced us to Brother and Sister Nebeker, an older couple who welcomed us into their home and seemed grateful to have our help.

Not more than a week after we arrived in our new home, I was out in the yard one day feeding clothes into a pot of boiling water. Hanna hurried up to me, her face radiating happiness as she delivered a piece of news that hit me like a fist. "Hakan asked me to marry him!" she said breathlessly, her blue eyes shining with joy.

I tried to smile, but it was forced. I bent to retrieve a shirt from the basket and stirred it into the pot with a long wooden pole. "Are you all right?" Hanna asked, leaning in closer to me.

"Why wouldn't I be?" I asked as I stirred the clothes around as hard as I could, pretending to be too busy to talk.

"Your eyes are watery. Is the steam too hot? Do you want me to take a turn?"

Hanna's concern only made me feel worse. "Yes," I said simply as I let go of the pole and hurried into the house. I shut myself into the room that I shared with Hanna and let my hot tears wash down my face.

I went to the wedding. I tried to see Hakan as a wicked troll, one who put ugly changeling babies into cradles after they snatched the human babies away. But as I watched him gaze tenderly at Hanna, I knew that any babies Hakan had anything to do with would be perfectly adorable, because they would be his.

I settled into my lonely life without Hanna or Hakan at the Nebeker's and tried to keep myself busy.

A week later, I answered a knock on the door to find Hakan staring at me as though he was a shipwrecked man desperate for a boat. "Please help me," he said. "Hanna's sick."

"I'll help," I said without even stopping to think about it. I grabbed my shawl and threw it over my shoulders as I followed him out the door. Hanna was lying in bed, her face pale and creased with pain. "Where does it hurt?" I asked as I touched her forehead.

"My stomach," she answered weakly. I got some water boiling. When it was ready, I dipped a clean cloth in it, cooled it enough to bear touching, then laid it across her abdomen.

"Have you called the doctor?" I asked Hakan.

"He's out," Hakan said. "They don't expect him back until late tonight." I stayed with Hanna until the doctor came, then refused Hakan's offer to walk me home. His place was beside his wife. I set off alone. As I turned up Nebeker's walk, I saw the distinctive hunched figure of Hakan standing almost a block away. When I reached the door, he turned and headed back the way he had come.

The doctor couldn't find any remedy that helped Hanna's stomach pains. They just got worse and worse. I felt exhausted at the end of each day from just sitting with her. Her pain hurt me, and her distress was heavy on my heart. I'd never met her before our ocean voyage, and now it seemed as though I'd known her forever. She was my friend, and I prayed that she would soon be healed from her misery.

Two days later, Hanna died. As I sat beside her still and quiet body, tears coursed down my cheeks. Although it hadn't come in the way I had wanted, nevertheless, I said a silent prayer thanking Father in Heaven for Hanna's release from the terrible pain.

A few days after the funeral, Hakan came to call. "How are you?" I asked him gently.

"Come sit with me on the porch," he said. I settled myself on the bench and he sat beside me. He seemed to be gathering his thoughts, and I waited a few moments for him to speak. "Sissla, I do believe the Lord has a sense of humor," he said finally.

I gave a start of surprise. "What?" I asked.

"In thirty seven years I never found a girl that I wanted to marry. Then in one summer, I found two."

"Two?" I repeated.

"I loved you both," Hakan said simply.

"You love me?" I whispered.

Hakan didn't answer directly. "I didn't know at the time why I felt I should ask Hanna to marry me first, but I trusted the promptings of the spirit. Now I know why."

"Poor Hanna," I said, my heart aching with the loss. "She was so young to die."

"The Lord knows more than we," Hakan said. "Hanna's in a better place. But we're still here. Sissla, I'd like you to be my wife."

My thoughts spun as the silence stretched between us. Thoughts of Hakan on the trek chased each other around in my head. His patience with Sister Belnap and his willingness to walk so she could ride, his tenderness with orphaned Aggie, his joy of dancing even at the end of a hard day of travel, and his sincere efforts to make everyone feel wanted.

"Sissla?" Hakan said uncertainly. "Will you marry me?"

I was flooded with warm certainty when I recalled what Hanna had said from the first. A good, kind man was worth more than a man who was merely good looking. I loved Hakan, my funny, tender-hearted prince. Aggie would have been thrilled with the ending to this story. Well, I'd just have to tell the stories to my own children.

My voice came out all wobbly when I said, "Yes, I will."

Hakan squeezed my hand. "You're beautiful, you know." I laughed. I actually felt beautiful. So we were married. Our third child was a daughter, and we named her Hannah.

*Mary Seamons tells the story of Peter Anderson taking care of his sixteen-year-old sister Johanna on the trek across the plains. Peter gave Johanna's precious new red coat, made for her by her mother, to the Indians in order to pacify them. Johanna didn't know it was gone until she saw one of the Indians wearing her coat and found her trunk empty.*

The Hakan Anderson Families history book tells the story of Hakan who was sent back across the plains from Utah in 1863 to help other settlers find their way. He was put in charge of two young women and their older chaperone. Both Hanna Nelson and Cecelia (Sissla) Swenson fell in love with Hakan. He first married Hanna, who died three weeks later. Then he proposed to Sissla who happily agreed to the union. They named one of their daughters Hannah.

# DANDY ON A DONKEY

Ed must have been soft in the head. Didn't he know that you don't come courting riding on a donkey? I was an older and wiser twenty-four-year old, so I knew these things. I was also unmarried, but that was beside the point.

Ed kneed his donkey into a trot. He couldn't urge him along with his heels because his heels were nearly dragging on the ground. "Hello, Will!" Ed called cheerfully as he pulled to a stop in front of me and easily stepped off his barrel-bellied mount. I smiled as much from amusement as in greeting. His frock coat was dusty, his trousers crumpled. Perched on his head was a ridiculous little hat that looked like a turtle with its limbs pulled in.

"So, Ed, you've come on a donkey to make a good impression on my sister?" I asked, running my hand over the little donkey's head. The animal patiently bore my touch.

"Oho," Ed grinned, shaking a finger at me. "Methinks you're disparaging my fine steed. I'll have you know that Jasper here had enough courage to escape the Indians when they stole our horses last week. He was the sole survivor, found wandering down the mountainside after his narrow escape."

"Maybe they let him go on purpose," I said.

Ed's eyes shifted past me. "Glory be," he murmured, "How many sisters do you have?"

I glanced over my shoulder to see several girls of various sizes flocking to the porch railing. "Well, at last count I had sixteen," I boasted.

Ed's eyes widened. Then he quickly brushed his palms down the front of his coat. "Here comes Rosalia," he said. Rosalia had been with me when I'd gone to Nephi and first met Ed, who was clerking at the general store. She'd asked him the price on a bolt of fabric, and he'd stuttered so badly she must have thought he was addled. When Rosalia had wandered across the store and become absorbed in examining a new shipment of hats stacked on a table in the corner, Ed took me aside and asked if he could come calling.

41

I'd told him the more the merrier.

Now here he was, looking as addled as ever in his rumpled finery. "Hello, Edward," Rosalia said, as bold as a rooster. I raised my eyebrows at her.

Ed tipped his hat with a flourish, which was a mistake. A seam of sweaty dust had gathered around his hatband and showed plain across his forehead like a stripe on a coon's tail. "Miss Cox," he greeted her.

My sister laughed. "Call me Rosalia," she admonished him. Ed's face reddened as he replaced his hat and nodded. "We've got some supper ready," Rosalia said, clasping her hands behind her back and twisting back and forth at the waist so that the hem of her long skirt nearly brushed Ed's shoes.

Ed grinned. "I'll just take care of Jasper and be right in," he assured her.

I clamped my hand firmly on Ed's shoulder. "After he helps us do chores," I added.

"Sure, Will, glad to," he answered heartily, following me toward the barn.

Ed turned Jasper out into the pasture to graze before he did his share of milking and feeding the livestock. The pasture was about gone, since autumn was crawling down the mountain slopes further each day, coloring the trees red and gold and nipping the grass back until there was just enough for one small donkey.

In spite of his dusty finery, Ed worked steadily and cheerfully to help get the chores done. I had to wonder if it was his normal work habit, or if it was just so he could get in to the supper table and the female company sooner.

As we climbed up the porch steps, I admonished Ed, "Careful not to spill any soup on those dandy duds of yours."

"Not to worry," Ed replied confidently. "I just got back from a trek to Missouri. While I was back east, I learned how to eat with all the proper utensils and even the right moment to lift my pinkie in the air." He crooked his little finger and tilted his head with a silly smile. I chuckled. "I even learned about the latest fashions," Ed said, clutching his lapels in both hands. "Missouri's where I got this hat." He ran his fingers around the thin brim. I didn't bother telling Ed that was nothing to brag about. "I know my manners," he declared.

Ed more than proved his words. He charmed all of my sisters until they were giggling and tossing admiring glances at him. Even my little brothers seemed impressed, and I noticed that a couple of them were trying to copy his mannerisms. My sisters, mother, and aunts seemed especially fascinated to hear news from back east.

"There are people everywhere," Ed said, spreading his hands apart.

"Kind of like this table?" I quipped. My sister Louisa shushed me.

"How are the girls wearing their hair?" Lovina asked.

Will answered quickly, "On their heads." My little brothers burst out laughing, and I had to cover a smile.

"Edward!" Rosalia scolded him gently in rebuke.

"It depends on the age of the girl," Ed said with a shrug. "Someone like little Calista here," Ed pointed to my six-year-old sister, "would be wearing braids or ringlets. A lady like you, on the other hand," Ed looked at Lovina who blushed prettily, "might pull it up soft and full around her face, with a knot pinned at the top."

"Oh, that sounds pretty," Eliza said dreamily, her chin on her hand.

"It's no prettier than yours," Ed said sincerely. Eliza's hand flew up to her hair as a look of pure delight spread across her face.

Rosalia threw Eliza an impatient look before she scooted her chair closer to Ed, leaned her elbow on the table and said, "Will you show us the latest dance steps?"

"I'd need someone to dance with first," Ed said slyly.

"There's no music, Rosalia," Eliza said, exasperated.

My sister Therissa spoke up, "What kind of dresses are they wearing?" she asked as Rosalia and Eliza glared at each other across the table.

Ed leaned back in his chair and put his hands as far apart as he could. "They're wearing hoops so big that the skirts look like bells when the ladies walk." My little sisters giggled behind their hands. "They've got fitted sleeves to the wrist and small, white collars right up to the neck.

"What color are they?" Mary asked timidly.

Ed shrugged, "All colors."

"What color do you like best?" Eliza teased him.

"Green," Ed answered quickly as Eliza fingered the sleeve of her dark green dress.

"Are the girls in St. Louis pretty?" Rosalia asked boldly.

Ed shrugged. "They're just girls, same as you."

"I'll bet their hands are softer than ours," Lovina said wistfully as she rubbed one of her palms with a finger.

"Soft as dough and twice as squishy," Ed said, making a face. All my sisters giggled, and Ma smiled.

"Sing us some of the latest songs," Eliza begged.

"Yes, sing them to us," Rosalia teased, leaning forward on her elbows.

I didn't particularly care to hear Ed singing. Besides, the farmhands in the barn would be waiting for their supper. I'd probably stayed too long all ready. I stood up and excused myself, urging Ed to stay and fill the ladies in on all the latest news. Ma followed me to the kitchen and helped me load up a supper tray.

On my way to the barn, I noticed old Jasper standing patiently by the pasture gate. "Sorry, fella, this isn't for you," I said. Jasper nibbled on the top gate pole as I shouldered my way into the men's quarters. One of the hands named Gardner asked, "Is that Ed fellow still eating?"

"Eating up the female attention," I grinned as I set the tray down on a table.

"He looks sissified to me," Haslam grumbled, pulling back a chair. It was no secret that Has was sweet on Rosalia.

Titus said in a high voice, batting his eyelashes like a girl, "That's just because of all the lovey-dovey stars in his eyes." He looked so ridiculous I couldn't help laughing.

"You enjoy your supper," I chuckled. "I'll be back in a bit." Titus shrugged and dug in to the sweet potatoes. "You'd better bless that," I reminded him. "Rosalia was in the kitchen." I took satisfaction in seeing Haslam's ears turn red before I let myself out into the cool autumn evening.

When I got back a good half hour later I said, "I'm ready to turn in."

"Wait a bit," Haslam said looking at me slyly. "We ought to give Romeo a proper welcome when he takes leave of the ladies. We don't want him crying hisself to sleep over a lonely heart, now, do we?" I shrugged as Has looked out the small window that faced the house. "Here he comes!" he called, drawing back. He took hold of the handle on the pistol he wore at his side. Most of the hired men wore their clothes to bed in order to be ready at a moment's notice for any emergency. Some even slept with their guns on, always ready to defend farm and family against Indians, rustlers, or other enemies. I wondered with a small flash of alarm if Haslam considered Ed to be an enemy. I couldn't believe he would be jealous just because Ed had entertained a bunch of girls, half of them under ten years old.

I heard the latch slide open and turned to see Ed's smiling face appear in the doorway just one second before a deafening gunshot boomed. Ed dropped to the floor. "Hey!" I yelled in alarm as I gripped Haslam's shoulder. His smoking pistol was clutched in his hand. I was too late.

I stared in horror as Ed struggled to reach his pistol from its holster underneath his city coat. I scanned his body for blood, but didn't see any. "What are you trying to do?" Ed yelled as he stood up, pistol in hand, his back against the wall as he glared at first Has, then me.

I grabbed Haslam's arm that still held the smoking gun. "What's wrong with you?" I yelled.

"Spider," Has answered with a smirk. "Could have been a black widow. Didn't want our guest to get poison-bit and go home in a coffin." Ed turned warily to examine the bullet hole in the doorframe as Haslam holstered his gun. Has sniffed loudly. "What's that smell?" he asked.

"Gunpowder," I said through clenched teeth.

"Smells like a dandy to me," Has said.

"He helped do chores," I defended Ed. "There's some manly odor mixed in with the perfume."

"Perfume from sitting by the ladies," Gardner grinned.

"You're lucky to have such beautiful sisters," Ed sighed, holstering his gun and moving toward an empty bunk.

"We're not all blood relatives," Has reminded him pointedly.

"Yeah." Ed flopped down on the bunk. "Me neither. I'm beat. I'm not used to so many females talking to me all at once. Trying to answer all their questions wore me out."

"Not man enough," Has muttered as I blew out the lamp.

Ed's yelling woke me up the next morning. "Will! They stole him again!"

I sat up in bed. "What?" I asked, forcing my eyes open. "Who?"

"The Indians took Jasper!"

"No!" I said. "If they'd been here, someone would have raised the alarm."

"They're sneaky," Will declared. "If they want to, they can come and go and you don't even know it."

I shook my head. "Maybe Jasper just wandered off in search of greener pastures."

"You've gotta help me find him," Ed pleaded.

I raised my eyebrows and shook my head. "I don't know, Ed, I've got to go in the canyon today and cut wood."

"Please, Will, how'm I going to get home without Jasper? It's better than forty miles!"

I swung my legs over the edge of my bunk. "Tell you what. You come with me to cut wood and I'll help you look for Jasper in the mountains." Ed looked doubtful. "That's where you found him the last time," I reminded him.

"All right," Ed answered reluctantly.

Ed seemed rather sullen at breakfast, even though he was the first one served with biscuits and jam and was kept supplied with cold milk and corn mush. The molasses jar was always being scooted in close to his plate. I noticed Lovina walking slowly, her head balanced as carefully as a ball on a stick. Her hair was pulled up loosely, making it puff out around her face. Instead of the close braids she usually wore, there was a round ball of hair pinned at the top of her head. She looked like a different girl, and I wasn't sure I liked the difference.

Ed sat solemnly beside me in the wagon as we rode away from the house toward the mountains for wood. He barely acknowledged the female voices that called cheery goodbyes to him. Every so often he'd turn his head this way and that, his eyes scanning the landscape. I figured he was looking for Jasper. With the nip of autumn in the air, we kept ourselves good and warm by chopping up the skeletal deadwood lying in between the standing timber. Ed cut his share, even though he paused every half hour or so to call, "Jasper!" and peer in between the tree trunks. His donkey never showed so much as one long ear all day.

With the wagon full and the sun low in the sky, we headed down the mountain. Ed slumped dejectedly in the seat beside me. As we turned the bend in the road that brought my house into view, I said, "Maybe he walked home."

"Your house or mine?" Ed asked sourly. The sun was all but gone over the west mountains with just a few golden fingers sliding along the house and barn before slipping off the edge of the world. Ed suddenly jumped to his feet in the moving wagon. "Jasper!" he yelled.

Haloed in the light of the setting sun was Jasper. The donkey was standing nearly as high as our barn roof, perched on top of the new straw stack that was piled up against the barn wall. There was a lumpy burlap sack perched on the donkey's back. A length of twine had been tied a couple of feet from the top of the sack, fashioning a crude head. When I'd made the burlap man the night before, he was sitting up straight, but now he was tipped sideways over Jasper's back on his lonely ride to nowhere.

As soon as I slowed the wagon, Ed was out of the seat and scrambling up the straw stack. He moved much faster than I had when I'd followed the same route the night before with a reluctant Jasper at the end of a rope. I watched Ed reach his patient donkey and untie him from a rafter of the barn roof. He pulled off the burlap man and tossed him aside. Then Ed and Jasper came sliding down the small straw mountain and headed for the barn door. "We found him!" I yelled exultantly to Ed's retreating back. He didn't bother to turn around.

At supper, I noticed that at least half my sisters had their hair pulled up into single knots like Lovina's. They looked like they were wearing popovers on their heads. Every one of them had their Sunday dresses on, too. They tried to draw Ed into conversation, but his answers were short and to the point. He wasn't nearly as charming as he had been the night before.

Ed left when I did, carrying the basket of rolls when I took the men's supper out to the barn. "I don't suppose you know anything about Jasper being tied on top of the straw stack?" he asked me.

"I suppose I do," I admitted.

Ed was quiet a moment before he said, "I'll give you thanks for leaving him a bucket of water."

"My heartfelt thanks in return for all the wood you helped me get," I replied jovially. Ed gave a single snort of humorless laughter, then opened the barn door and stepped well back to let me go through first. I imagined he was worried about another spider on the doorjamb.

Ed and Jasper were gone when I got up in the morning. He hadn't said a word to anyone about leaving. I had to face my sisters alone and give them the news. All of their faces dropped with keen disappointment, and Lovina's face crumpled into tears.

"You played a mean prank!" Rosalia scolded me.

"It didn't hurt Jasper any," I defended myself.

"You hurt Edward's feelings!" Eliza declared. "He thinks we hate him!"

48

"Oh, no, he doesn't think you girls hate him," I assured her.

"How do you know?" Rosalia demanded.

"The first night he was here, he said all of you were beautiful."
To my surprise, two more of my sisters broke into tears.

"We never heard him say that!" Rosalia said, her eyes sparking.

Eliza bayoneted me with her eyes and I took in Ma's stern gaze
before I replied, "He said it out in the barn!"

"You are more of a beast than Jasper!" Rosalia spat before she
turned on her heel.

"Why?" I held my hands out in confusion. "Because Ed said
you were beautiful?"

"Because you scared him off," Eliza sniffed.

"So I'll invite him back," I said. "I'll take all the blame!" In
spite of my attempts to make peace, I finally decided to take my
breakfast out on the porch. The cold autumn morning felt warmer
than a kitchen full of women with bad tempers.

The next time I went to Nephi I made a point to go into the
general store. Ed was coming back to visit no matter what, even if
I had to hog tie him and carry him back. My sisters were counting
on it.

I didn't see Ed behind the counter, so I spoke to the middle
aged man in the white apron who was sliding bottles of liniment
into place on the shelf. "Excuse me. Could I please speak to Ed?"

He turned toward me. "Sorry, young man," he said as he
looked at me over the tops of his spectacles. "Ed doesn't work here
any more. He's moved to St. Louis."

*In a story reported by Norma Wanlass from the autobiography of
Will Arthur Cox, a young man named Ed from a distant town came to
woo one of Will's sisters somewhere around the year 1863. The only
mount available to him was a donkey that escaped from an Indian horse
raid. All of the girls got gussied up for the visitor, and made him the center of attention as he recounted the sights of his recent trip back East.*

The boys, feeling left out, helped Will pull Ed's donkey up on top of the straw stack. One of the hired hands also shot at a knot in the ceiling when Ed walked into the men's quarters in the barn. Ed dropped to the floor and drew his gun before he realized it was all a jest.

Unable to find his steed the next morning, Ed was persuaded to help Will get a load of wood from the mountains where Will promised to help Ed look for his donkey. When they returned from their day of work, Ed noticed the donkey on the straw stack and brought him down. Although he spent the night, Ed was gone the next morning before anyone else got up.

# 6.
# LETTING LUCY DOWN EASY

I didn't realize how much I loved Mary Ellen until the day she told me that Bishop Snow had asked her father for her hand in marriage. My heart stopped. "What did your father say?" I asked.

Mary Ellen turned her big, beautiful eyes up to me and said, "Pa told him that he doesn't want me to be a plural wife." My heart gave a joyful leap and began beating again. Mary Ellen smiled demurely at me. "Bishop Snow was quite put out, even though Pa assured him it was nothing personal. He just didn't want me wed to a man who's already married."

"I agree," I said fervently. "You deserve someone who can devote his full attention to you." I decided at that very moment that I was ready to give up Betsy, Eunice, and all the other girls so I could court Mary Ellen. Having almost lost her to Bishop Snow, I knew with certainty that she was the one I wanted for my wife.

I determined that the perfect opportunity to tell all the young ladies of my intentions would be at the community dance on Friday. I would ask each girl for a final dance and tell her how I could no longer hope to keep her for myself, but had to let her go to bless the life of some other lucky fellow. I figured they'd all be understanding and eventually get over it, except maybe Lucy.

Lucy Allen was a good-natured girl who laughed too loudly and talked too much for my taste. She was the first to greet me when I went to a social function, boldly seizing my arm like a morning glory blossom winding itself around a corn stalk. Morning glories are pretty, but if unchecked, they choke off the growth of the plant they're so eager to embrace. If I were to let Lucy down at the dance, she could very well cause a scene, which was something I wanted to avoid.

When I arrived at the dance I found that I couldn't avoid Lucy even if I'd wanted to. As the other unoccupied young women stood talking among themselves or helped arrange the refreshment table, Lucy hurried up to me and took my arm. "Hello, Fred," she gushed.

"Hello, Lucy," I answered as I walked her toward the dancers. I figured that the quickest way to rid myself of Lucy would be to dance with her once, then excuse myself to ask some of the others. As we stepped onto the floor, Bishop Snow caught my eye. He was dancing with one of his wives. I wasn't sure which one. He nodded a greeting to me and let his glance take in Lucy before he moved off into the crowd.

I thought about talking to Lucy of my intentions while we danced, but she didn't give me a chance. She chattered on and on about her family and her new dress and the last social we'd both been to so that my ears were ringing by the time the fiddler stopped. Before he could strike up another tune, I led Lucy firmly over to the sidelines. "Thank you, Lucy," I said. I immediately turned to Eunice. "May I have this dance?" I asked with a slight bow. Eunice blushed and put her hand into my outstretched one.

When I told Eunice that I needed to let her go from my life but that I would always cherish her friendship, she looked first confused, then chagrined. I thanked her sincerely when the dance ended. I escorted her back to her place where she was soon claimed for a dance with another young man. I was glad to see her smiling at him as they moved around the dance floor.

I made my way through all the girls I had flirted with, doing my best to let them down gently. Eventually I'd spoken to all the girls except Lucy. I easily put the problem of Lucy out of my mind as I took a blissful turn on the dance floor with Mary Ellen. I noticed Bishop Snow again, this time with a different wife. He looked closely at us as we made our way around the floor. He smiled at Mary Ellen, who ducked her head and averted her eyes. I fervently hoped that Bishop Snow understood Brother Tuttle's wishes regarding Mary Ellen's future husband. I certainly did.

I'd lost count of the dances I'd had with Mary Ellen when I felt a tap on my shoulder. "May I have a dance with the most beautiful girl here?" I turned to see Brother Tuttle smiling at me. Mary Ellen's father was a big man, and I stepped aside so he could move into my place.

"It will soon be time for me to take my post for midnight guard duty at the fort," I told them. "So I'll bid you good night."

Mary Ellen's eyes held steady on mine. "Good night, Fred," she said softly. My heart thrilled. I would look forward to a life-time of hearing those words.

I wandered over to the side of the dance pavilion, stealing glances at Mary Ellen as she danced with her father. I felt certain that he would approve of me as a son-in-law.

A hand took hold of my arm and slid snugly into the crook of my elbow. I was familiar with that grasp, and wasn't surprised to glance down and see Lucy there, her head nearly leaning on my shoulder. I decided to get the unpleasantness over with. "Lucy, I need to talk to you," I said.

"What about, Fred?" she asked, looking up at me with eyes so full of hope and expectation that I knew this wasn't going to be easy.

"I really care ..." I began.

"Let's walk out to where the music isn't so loud," Lucy said, tugging at my arm. I reluctantly followed her down a narrow path leading to the creek that was flowing with new spring runoff a short distance from the dance floor. A wooden footbridge spanned the water. Lucy stopped walking when we reached the center of the bridge. She leaned on the railing and gazed into the water as it gurgled around rocks and branches hanging over into the streambed.

I had just opened my mouth to speak again when Lucy's voice rose above the noise of the water. "I'm going up north this summer to work." Then she stood and faced me, her head tilted and her eyes shining in the moonlight. "That is, unless something happens to keep me here," she continued hopefully.

She had just presented the perfect solution to my problem. I jumped at the chance to let Lucy down easy. "Well, I'm sure you'll do just fine," I assured her heartily. "There will be a lot of people up there your age, lots of dances and parties and all sorts of new experiences."

Lucy's eyes had lost some of their shine, but her voice contin-ued stoically, "Aunt Mary says I could get a housekeeping position. Brother Tanner's wife died of childbed fever, and he needs some-one to care for his children."

"You'd be very good at that," I encouraged her. She dropped her head and stared at the bridge. I didn't want her to start crying just because I hadn't begged her to stay. I couldn't read her expression with her head down. I hoped she could understand that she just wasn't my type.

Heavy footsteps sounded on the bridge behind me. I turned to see Bishop Snow approaching. "Well, well, young lovers!" The bishop said amiably. "Taking advantage of the moonlight?"

I felt a shiver go through me when the bishop called us lovers. He was known for his sense of humor, and did have a tendency to tease, so I shrugged it off. "When are you two getting married?" he continued jovially.

"Oh, he hasn't asked me yet," Lucy said quickly. She made a pout with her lips. "If he doesn't soon make up his mind, I'm going to think he doesn't want me!" She took hold of my arm and looked up at me with moonlit eyes.

"Well, how about it Fred?" the bishop asked. "How about if I perform a little ceremony right now?" The humor in his voice was unmistakable.

"Oh, I'd like that," Lucy said softly, her forlorn words nearly lost in the rippling of the stream. This jest of Bishop Snow's could play right into my plans. It would obviously mean a lot to Lucy to have the memory of a pretend ceremony. Then she could go up north and I'd be guilt-free to pursue Mary Ellen.

"Yes, all right," I said off-handedly, letting the bishop know that I was going along with his joke.

Without any other preamble, Bishop Snow said, "Do you, Lucy Allen, take this man Fred W. Cox Junior to be your husband until death do you part, to love, honor, and obey?"

"I do," Lucy said with fervor.

"Do you, Fred Cox Junior, take Lucy Allen to be your wife and helpmate 'til death do you part, to love and cherish her?" I opened my mouth to reply, but no sound came out.

Bishop Snow's voice prompted me, "Well, do you?"

"Sure," I said quickly. "Now, if you'll excuse me, I've got guard duty." I turned to Lucy, her face staring up at me with all the devotion of a faithful dog. "Goodbye, Lucy. Good luck in the big city." I turned and walked away.

That summer was idyllic. I didn't hear anything from Lucy, and Mary Ellen and I spent as much time together as possible. Her parents heartily approved of me. We made plans for a fall wedding, after the harvest was in. When the time was right, I made an appointment with Bishop Snow. He ushered me into his parlor and motioned me to sit down.

"Now, Fred, what can I do for you?" he asked.

"I'd like an interview for a recommend to get married," I told him.

Bishop Snow pulled his eyebrows together in an uncharacteristically stern look. "Fred, do you feel you have the means to support two wives?" he asked.

I felt a jolt of surprise. Perhaps he hadn't understood me. "No, Bishop, I'm not marrying two wives, I'm only marrying one. Mary Ellen Tuttle," I explained.

"Fred, is your memory so short?" the bishop asked me. "I married you and Lucy Allen last spring."

My mouth dropped open in disbelief. "But that was all in jest," I managed to say.

"Is that what you thought?" Bishop Snow asked, raising his eyebrows. "I don't take the sanctity of marriage lightly, and neither should you," he said.

"But the words you said," I began.

"Were all perfectly legal," he finished for me.

"I thought you were only humoring Lucy," I protested.

"You agreed to it," he reminded me, no trace of humor on his face.

"But surely you can just erase it. We've never even been together. I haven't even seen her since that night."

"What's done is done," Bishop Snow said solemnly.

I left Bishop Snow's house in a frenzy. He couldn't be serious.

I rushed home and spilled out the story to my parents. They in turn took me to call on the Tuttles. When Mary Ellen was summoned to the room and heard the Bishop's declaration, she cried so hard it about broke my heart.

It was decided to bring the Allens in on the discussion, since their daughter was involved, too. After everyone was gathered together, we decided to go in force to visit Bishop Snow and get the matter resolved. Even though we started out talking to him reasonably, he still wouldn't budge. His decision was final.

"You haven't heard the last of this," my father said when we left the bishop's house. As we headed toward home, my father declared, "We'll go to Salt Lake City for General Conference and talk to President Brigham Young himself. We'll get this straightened out, don't you worry."

With my heart on edge, I traveled to Salt Lake in the wagon beside my father, leaning forward the whole way as if that would make us get there faster. Pa set up an interview with the church president, stating that it was an emergency and we simply couldn't go back home without speaking to him. We had to wait until after the conference was over, so we stayed an extra day in the city. When we were finally ushered in to the president's office, I took courage from the smile he wore as he greeted us with a hearty handshake. He asked after our health and general questions about our settlement before he said, "Now, what is the pressing matter that you just had to see me about?"

I told Brigham Young my side of the story, and Pa filled in the details of our meeting with Bishop Snow. After we'd had our say, the president stood up and clasped his hands behind his back. Then he paced the room, his face grave as he thought deeply on what we had said. Suddenly he stopped, turned and pointed his finger at me, and said, "Young man, you are married. I suggest you take your wife home and make the best of it."

My mouth dropped open as my heart constricted. President Young said, "I bid you good day," and strode out of the room.

My father dropped his head. "I'm sorry, son," he mumbled. "I don't know what else to do."

I shrugged helplessly. "I guess we go fetch Lucy and I make the best of it." We both stood up and headed for the door. "I suppose it's my own fault for making light of a sacred ordinance," I said. "Marriage is no joke."

My father clapped a hand on my shoulder as I stepped outside. "Son, you are wise beyond your years," he said. We climbed in the buggy and headed down the road to pick up my wife.

*On April 20, 1857, Fred Cox Jr. went to a dance intent on informing the girls he had dated that he would no longer be available to court them because he had decided to marry Mary Ellen Tuttle. Mary Ellen's father had recently turned down Bishop Snow's proposal to take Mary Ellen as his plural wife.*

*Fred and a girl named Lucy Allen, who was particularly fond of him, stepped outside at intermission so he could break the news to her. When Lucy told Fred that she was going up north to work for the summer, Fred figured that he wouldn't have to break her heart after all. When Bishop Snow came along and jovially asked if they were ready to be married, Fred consented to the jest as a parting memory for Lucy to take with her.*

*Six months later when Fred's proposal was accepted by Mary Ellen, he went to Bishop Snow for a sealing recommend and was informed that he was already married to Lucy. Church President Brigham Young confirmed that the marriage was legal and valid.*

*Fred took his bride home and made the best of it, eventually fathering twelve children with Lucy. Fred eventually took two other wives.*

*Mary Ellen married Walter Stringham two years later and remained his only wife until her death in 1902.*

*This story comes from Fred's own son Howard, and was recorded by Norma Wanlass.*

# DISHING IT OUT

"Grandpa, shouldn't we give him a ride?" I asked as we drove our buggy past the thin man walking beside the road. A smile parted the man's long gray beard as he tipped his hat to us. Grandpa didn't even slow down, but merely raised a hand in greeting before he answered, "Brother Soder wouldn't accept."

"How do you know?"

"I've offered before. He always says no."

"Where's he going?"

"He's visiting his wives."

I crinkled up my forehead. "Don't they all live in the same house?" I asked.

Grandpa tipped his hat back. "They don't even live in the same town," he said.

"He must get tired," I said, looking back over my shoulder to watch Brother Soder get smaller and smaller as we pulled further ahead of him.

"We're aiming to fix that," Grandpa said as we passed the first tree in the row that bordered the road leading into town.

"How?" I said.

"We're holding a dance on Saturday for a fund raiser."

"What's a fund raiser?"

"That means you have to pay to get in and dance. The money that we make will be used to buy Brother Soder a horse," Grandpa said, turning down the road that led to his house.

My heart felt comforted that Brother Soder would not have to walk much longer. Grandpa pulled the buggy up beside the barn and I jumped down. I ran into the house where Grandmamma gave me a hug before she said I must be tired from the ride. How could I get tired from sitting down? It was Brother Soder who must get tired.

I didn't want to take a nap, but I knew better than to argue. I obediently climbed up onto Grandmamma's feather bed. As I settled my head into a pillow, Grandmamma swung a cloud-soft yellow shawl up over me. It drifted down over my arms and legs like lazy feathered birds and settled down into all the hollows. I drew my knees up and turned on my side, facing the bedroom door. Grandmamma left the door open just a little bit as she eased her way through.

I thought about sliding off the bed and peeking through the door, but the risk of getting caught was too great. Grandmamma wasn't mean, but she was firm. If you followed her rules, she was as jovial as the butcher Brother Gruder, who would slip trimmings to the poorer immigrants so they could have something to flavor their soup. If you didn't follow Grandmamma's rules, you were in for a scolding, and practicing the rule until you either got it right or dropped dead of exhaustion.

I woke to the sound of knocking. "What?" I said as my eyes popped open. There was no one at the bedroom door. I smelled food cooking. I could smell chicken, and biscuits. Threaded through the main course smells was something sweet, like cake, but it wasn't chocolate. I knew there would be a vegetable, perhaps beans that Grandmama would have picked from the garden while I was asleep. If she hadn't made me take a nap, I would have helped her. I was a good helper. That's why Mama let me come to Grandmamma's house.

Mama was in a family way. I think that meant she was sharing me with her family. Her tummy was big, like Brother Gruder's, but she didn't laugh as much as he did.

I rolled over on my stomach, swung my feet over the side of the bed and slid to the floor. I pushed the bedroom door wide just in time to see Grandmamma pulling open the front door.

"Brother Munk," Grandmamma said in her coolly polite voice. Her head was erect, the touch of gray on the sides of her upswept chestnut hair shining in the warm rays of the setting sun that found their way through the open door. She wasn't smiling as she moved back to let the visitor in.

"Sister Anderson!" Brother Munk answered cheerfully as he stepped into the room. I actually saw him sniff the air, which wasn't

SHIRLEY BAHLMANN

polite. I knew because Grandmamma had told me so once when she was baking.

"That's what dogs do," she'd told me firmly. "We are not dogs."

"Is Peter home?" Brother Munk said, slowly rubbing his hands together, although it wasn't the least bit cold.

"I was just going to call him for supper," Grandmamma said. She turned to me. "Wilma, go and get your Grandpa from outside."

"Yes, Ma'am," I said. Grandmamma knew I would need to use the privy after my nap. Sending me after Grandpa gave me a chance to go to the outhouse without announcing it to Brother Munk.

Grandpa was already headed toward the house. "Was that Brother Munk?" he asked me.

"Yes," I said, stepping from side to side as I paused to answer.

"Then it must be time for supper," Grandpa said, smiling. "He always seems to time his visits so that he can eat with us." Grandpa looked toward the house, and stuck his hands in his pockets. "It drives your Grandmamma to distraction."

"Yes, Sir," I said, crossing my legs.

"Let's go eat," he said, pulling his hand out of his pocket and holding it out to me.

"I can't yet," I said desperately, the urgency welling up inside me, "I have to…"

"You just take your time," Grandpa said. "I need to see how the apples are getting along." He turned his back to me as he sauntered over to the tree in the back yard. I hurried to take care of business, and then joined Grandpa.

We went around to the front door. "Hello, Erastus," Grandpa said when he saw Brother Munk standing by the mantel.

"Peter!" Brother Munk sounded relieved when he caught sight of Grandpa. "I've come to talk over some church business with you."

"Can you talk and eat at the same time?" Grandpa asked.

61

Before Brother Munk could answer, I said, "It's not polite to talk with your mouth full."

"I'll be careful of that," Brother Munk said.

"You must wash up first," I said, leading the way to the washbasin.

"Yes, Ma'am," Brother Munk said.

After Grandmamma's delicious chicken dinner, Grandpa and Brother Munk went into the parlor to talk while I helped Grandmamma clear up.

"Wilma, do you know why women live longer than men?" Grandmamma asked as she plunged her hands into the dishwater.

"No," I answered, piling more plates on the drain board beside her.

"It's because we always have things to do," Grandmamma replied. "We're always cooking something, cleaning something, washing something, or tending someone. Women are never done, and God won't call us home until our work on earth is done."

"Is Grandpa's work done?" I asked.

"It must be. He's sitting in the parlor with his feet up, talking to Brother Munk."

"But that's church work," I said.

"Yes, I suppose you could say that," Grandmamma said. She smiled at me, and then scrubbed vigorously at a pan.

I was relieved that Grandpa's work wasn't done yet. I didn't want him to die. "Is Brother Munk poor?" I asked.

Grandmamma turned to look at me with her eyebrows raised up. "Why do you ask that?" she said.

"He eats here a lot." I shrugged. "Maybe he doesn't have enough food. I could tell him that Brother Gruder would give him trimming scraps for free."

Grandmamma laughed loudly, then clapped her wet hand over her mouth in a most unladylike way. I lowered my eyebrows and looked at her sternly. She knew better than that.

Grandmamma wiped her hands and dried her face with her apron before she said, "Wilma, Brother Munk has more money than Grandpa. He just doesn't like to spend it."

I felt my eyes go wide with surprise. "You mean he has food and a house?"

"Yes," Grandmamma said. "A rather large house."

"Does he have a wife and kids, too?"

Grandmamma gave her head a shake. "No. He lives alone in his house, counting his money and watching the clock so he can go eat with other people and not have to cook for himself."

"Does he know how to cook?" I asked.

"I don't know," Grandmamma said, then waved her hand in the air as if she was shooing away a fly. "It makes no difference. We'll just share what we have when he comes, and thank the Lord there's enough and to spare."

"Brother Soder has lots of wives," I said.

Grandmamma looked at me curiously. "Some men do," she said.

"Maybe he would let Brother Munk have one," I said.

Grandmamma looked surprised before she shook her head. "That's not the way it works," she said. "Men don't share their wives. But I'll share these cookies with you!" Grandmamma wrapped some of her sugar cookies up in a clean dishtowel and handed them to me. "You bring that towel back next time you come," she said, kissing me on my forehead. As soon as Brother Munk left, Grandpa drove me home, but this time we didn't see Brother Soder.

Pa took me to the dance and paid a penny for me to get in. He was lucky that I went with him so he would have someone to dance with, because Mama didn't go. There were a lot of people there. I even had a turn to dance with Grandpa. I didn't even know that I fell asleep on the way home until I woke up in my bed, so I had to tell Mama about the dance the next morning.

When it was time for me to be part of the family way again, Grandpa picked me up at my house in his buggy. About halfway to Grandpa's house, I noticed Brother Soder. I had to look twice to make sure it was him, because this time he was sitting up high on a horse instead of walking along the road.

"Hello, Lars," Grandpa called. I waved. Brother Soder seemed reluctant to let go of the reins. He nodded a greeting to Grandpa, but he forgot to smile at me. He sat on the horse like it was a rolling log that might tip him off any minute.

As we rode past, I said, "Grandpa, that was so nice of you to help Brother Soder get a horse."

Grandpa chuckled. "Maybe his wives will appreciate having him around a little more."

Grandpa looked over at me, seeming to notice for the first time that I was carrying something on my lap. "Is that our dishtowel?"

I carefully picked up the folded white fabric. "Yes, it is," I said proudly, glad that I had remembered to bring it. "I even washed it myself, and I folded it, too, only see how the corners don't fit just right?" I tried to line up the corners a little neater without unfolding the towel. "I hope Grandmamma won't make me practice re-folding it."

Grandpa laughed. "She'll just be glad it's so clean," he said.

For some reason, I couldn't fall asleep when Grandmamma tucked me in for my nap. I couldn't even fall asleep by accident, even though I tried really hard. I kept my eyes closed for a long time, but my ears wouldn't stop working. Finally I rubbed my hair with my hands and twisted my dress around a little bit so it would look like I'd been asleep.

I took stumbly steps into the kitchen where Grandmamma was shelling peas. She looked at me with narrowed eyes. "Did you sleep?" she said sternly.

"My eyes were closed for a long time," I said, hoping she would think I had.

Grandmamma sighed. "You can help me shell peas if you don't fall asleep in the bucket." I happily settled down beside Grandmamma and got to work. Grandmamma was faster than I was. When she had enough, she put the pot on the stove and left me a handful from the bowl that I could eat fresh. She dumped the empty pods into the scrap bucket, which is where all the peelings and husks and the soft spots from apples went. Grandpa dumped the scrap bucket into the corral every day for the animals.

"The peas won't take long," Grandmamma said. "Go and get your grandpa to come wash for supper."

"Yes'm," I said.

Supper was fried ham, corn on the cob and fresh peas. It was delicious, as usual. Afterward I helped clear the table. I was using my nice clean dishtowel to wipe the dishes when a knock sounded on the door. Grandpa answered it.

"Hello, Brother Munk," I heard him say. Grandmamma plunked the last pan down into the water so hard that it splashed up onto her apron.

"Hello, Peter," Brother Munk said cheerfully.

"I'd invite you to supper, but we already ate," Grandpa said.

After a moment of silence, Brother Munk said slowly. "That's all right." It didn't sound like he meant it. I heard the short couch creak, and imagined that Grandpa had settled himself into it.

"Your apple tree looks bounteous," Brother Munk said.

"Yes, the blessings are flowing," Grandpa said. "We even raised enough money to get Brother Soder a horse. I don't remember seeing you at the dance, though."

"No, I couldn't make it," Brother Munk said. "I had other pressing business."

"You are a busy man," Grandpa said.

"Actually, I'm here today on an errand from the church leaders," Brother Soder said in a serious voice. "They have been discussing your situation, and feel that you are in a position to provide for a second wife."

Grandmamma stopped washing and stood as still as a hay derrick in winter.

Bother Munk continued, "Sister Freda Tobias is a recent immigrant, a young woman with a pleasant disposition and without prospects. We propose that you take her as your wife, shelter her, and raise up some children in righteousness."

Grandmamma moved faster than I'd ever seen her before. She snatched up her broom and dashed into the living room. When I finally scrambled down off my stool and hurried to the doorway, I was surprised to see Grandmamma hitting Brother Munk with the broom. He had his arms up as he struggled to stand up from his chair.

"You mind your own business, Erastus Munk!" she shouted. "You selfish man! Take a wife yourself before you go telling other men to take two!"

By this time, Brother Munk had made it to his feet. He ran for the door. Grandmamma followed him every step of the way, not resting her broom until Brother Munk had disappeared through the doorway. He didn't even stop to close it behind him.

What had gotten into Grandmamma? I stared at Grandpa in bewilderment. He caught my eye, then shrugged and winked a reassuring wink at me. Grandmamma closed the door with a bang. Grandpa hauled himself up off the couch and caught Grandmamma in his arms as she stormed back toward the kitchen.

"Elsie, you always did have a way with words," Grandpa said.

"Not in front of Wilma," Grandmamma said, pushing against Grandpa's chest. Grandpa kissed her cheek anyway before he let go. Grandmamma swished into the kitchen, and I heard the broom clatter back into its place in the corner.

"That's that," Grandpa said. "Are you ready to go home?" I was.

A few days later, Grandpa brought Grandmamma to my house. I was glad, because Mama was in bed making funny noises and looking sick. As Grandmamma swept into the bedroom with her satchel, I knew she would take care of Mama and make her better, so I climbed into the buggy beside Grandpa and we headed toward his house.

"Is Brother Munk sore?" I asked.

"I don't know," Grandpa smiled and shook his head. "He hasn't been back since you were there last."

After we'd traveled about a mile or so, I sat forward on the bench. "Grandpa, look, it's Brother Soder," I said, pointing at the familiar figure walking along beside the road.

Grandpa pulled his buggy to a stop beside Brother Soder. "Lars," he said, "What happened to your horse?"

Brother Soder looked up at us. "I sold it," he said cheerily.

Grandpa scratched his head. With a funny look on his face, he asked, "Why did you do that?

"I don't need a horse."

"But a horse will get you where you need to go a lot quicker."

Brother Soder stroked his beard absently. "I'm in no hurry. I have plenty of time."

"Well, well," Grandpa said as he eased back against the buggy seat. "I guess we should have asked you if you even wanted a horse before we went and got you one."

"Yup," Brother Soder agreed.

Grandpa cocked his head at Brother Soder and said, "If you don't mind my asking, what did you do with the money you got for the horse?"

Brother Soder lifted one foot and pulled up his pant leg. "Bought me a new pair of shoes," he said.

*Ernest J. Scow's father told him the story of a man he knew who walked between towns to visit his three wives. The community held a fund-raiser dance to raise enough money to buy the fellow a horse. A week later, as he was walking along the road, a neighbor stopped to ask the man where his horse was. He replied that he'd sold it because he didn't need a horse. He had plenty of time.*

*Wilma Morley Despain's family history tells of the time her grand-mother Elsie Margaret Poulson Anderson chased a bachelor from her home when he had the audacity to counsel her husband Peter to take a second wife some time around the 1870's.*

# 'TIL DEATH DO US PART

I'd first felt the cold premonition of fear ten years ago when I was six and my brother Jens was eight. I'd complained to Ma about the odd pain. She'd doctored me with poultices and awful tasting medicine, but the foreboding stayed with me until Jens died suddenly the next day. After that, the cold tightness had twisted around into aching loss, leaving me bereft of my brother and friend, lonely as I assumed the role of oldest boy in the family.

The frightening premonition had visited me again seven years later on a brittle winter day so cold and frozen that my favorite horse, Dancer, slipped on the ice and fell. Pa had found her out in the pasture, moaning and snorting in pain, a broken leg flopping pitifully as she flailed her three good legs so deeply into the snow that chunks of dark, frozen ground scattered around her like ashes. There was nothing to do but put her out of her misery. The single shot to her head caused two deaths, since Dancer was carrying a foal.

I'd crawled into bed the night Dancer was put down feeling that somehow Jens' and Dancer's deaths were my fault. If I had been warned that they were going to die, wasn't there something I could have done about it? The next morning, my heart felt as though it matched the frozen tree branch that tapped forlornly on my window. I couldn't stop myself from weeping with the pain of loss. I didn't notice my sister Elizabeth slip inside my room until she said softly, "Johan? Are you crying?"

I'd ducked my head down to wipe my eyes on the quilt. "No," I said, my blunt answer muffled by the thick fabric. I would never admit that I was crying to my eleven-year-old sister. "Go away," I said without looking up.

"Are you sick?"

"No." Elizabeth was quiet for so long, I thought she'd gone.

When I pulled my face out of the covers, she was still there, looking at me with eyes full of compassion. "I know you feel bad about what happened to Dancer yesterday." I didn't respond.

"Mama said we could go skating after we do our chores," Elizabeth said hopefully. I didn't smile at her before she left my room, even though my heart lifted a little at the thought of ice-skating.

Later that afternoon we gathered our skates and made our way to the frozen lake. Elizabeth and I weren't the first ones there. Several people were sliding across the ice in various stages of expertise; some gliding along in swoops and circle, others moving cautiously with feet angled together like a knock-kneed calf just learning how to walk. We found a log to sit on. I had just begun strapping on my skates when someone thumped my back, jarring my fingers so that I had to start all over. "Elizabeth!" I yelled, thinking she had done it just to slow me down so that I wouldn't get onto the ice before her.

"Hey, Johan, why the long face?" Seventeen-year-old Peter Ludvigson grinned down at me as he pulled his hand away.

"Why's your face so short?" I shot back at him as his brown mutt, Shag, stuck his nose under my hand, begging to be petted. I pushed him away from me. "Git!" I commanded, but Shag just danced around behind me and planted his front feet on the log, stretching his muzzle up as he tried to lick my face.

"Get down, Shag!" Peter ordered his dog. Shag hurried happily back to his master's side. "You're a funny man, Johan," Peter laughed, his voice warm and welcome. He had helped to fill the gap in my life that Jens had left. Peter was my closest friend.

Peter glanced over at my sister. "Elizabeth, do you need help?" he asked before he knelt down at her feet. In spite of Shag's eagerness to help, too, Peter quickly fastened her skates.

"Thank you," Elizabeth said, rubbing Shag behind his ears as she threw a coy glance up at Peter with her wide blue eyes.

"Glad to be of assistance," Peter said, standing up and holding out his hand. "May I have this dance?"

Elizabeth giggled and put her hand in Peter's. "Certainly you may, Brother Ludvigson, kind sir," she answered, trying to sound proper but merely sounding ridiculous. I was fussing with my second skate as my best friend led my sister onto the ice, Peter's step steady while Elizabeth wobbled as though her ankles were full of marbles. Shag stepped cautiously onto the icy surface until Peter order him to stay. Then Shag ran back to help me with my skates.

When I finally made my way onto the ice, Peter and Elizabeth were holding hands as they slid in and out among the other skaters. It took me awhile to find my balance on the ice. If I'd had someone older and taller to hold onto, I'd skate as good as Elizabeth, too. Not that I wanted to hold hands with Peter or anything. It certainly didn't help my balance any when other kids started to pelt me with snowballs. Yelling at them to stop only made them throw more, and started Shag barking. I teetered back over to the log and sat down. Shag quieted and sat beside me, staring out at the ice and his master. I decided I really wasn't in the mood for skating anyway.

I moved over to the bonfire to warm my toes. Before long I was ready to go home, and looked out onto the ice to find Elizabeth so I could tell her. That's when I heard the scream. The skaters turned their heads toward the sound, some digging their blades into the ice in order to slow down enough to stop. A girl screamed again and pointed to her sister sitting on the ice holding her ankle. "She can't get up!"

Peter darted through the skaters standing around uncertainly. He was the first one to reach the injured girl's side. He knelt and boldly took hold of her ankle. I could see the girl grimace and nod to Peter. He helped her up, and with another fellow on the other side of her, she limped over to the fire. Shag followed along behind them, whining in sympathy. No one seemed to feel very jolly after that, and the skating party broke up. Yet a spark had been kindled on that cold day between my sister and my best friend. During the three years that had passed since then, I knew that Peter's affections had grown to the point that he was now coming over mainly to see Elizabeth instead of me. It was obvious that Elizabeth returned his affection.

Suddenly impatient with myself for lying around and reminiscing when the cold fear was gripping my heart yet again, I kicked off my covers and stepped out of bed. Maybe I could figure out what the premonition was for and prevent disaster. After all, I was an older and wiser sixteen-year-old now. I hurriedly dressed and went downstairs. Elizabeth was standing at the stove with a gathered white apron tied at her waist as she turned over golden brown abelskivvers. The little round pancakes full of applesauce were cooked in a pan with hollows the size of eggs shaped into the metal surface. The hot, appley smell made my stomach rumble.

Elizabeth turned to look at me, and smiled teasingly. "Hi, sleepyhead," she said. I tried to smile back. Elizabeth's smile faded, and I was struck by how much she looked like our mother. At four-teen, she was fast maturing into a young lady, and a pretty one at that. There were lots of young men who would vie for her hand if my best friend hadn't already claimed it. Ma had made it plain that she didn't want Elizabeth married before she was fifteen. With her birthday coming up, I had noticed some new pillowslips lying around the house with needles full of colorful thread stuck into the fabric, waiting for female hands to return and work them into birds and flowers. There was a new quilt stretched on the frame. I'd caught Elizabeth humming to herself as she plied her needle in and out of the layers of fabric. This dowry would go with Elizabeth when she set up housekeeping after she became Mrs. Ludvigson.

"Are you all right?" Elizabeth asked me, a frown of concern on her forehead.

"Sure," I said, shrugging my shoulders as I sat down and plunked my elbows on the table. I folded my arms to shield my cold heart from Elizabeth's scrutiny.

"See how pretty I am!" a small voice rang through the kitchen as our little sister Marie came prancing in, a dress billowing out around her four-year-old legs as she twirled around in a wobbly cir-cle. I recognized the dress as one that had belonged to Elizabeth. Ma must have cut it down for Marie.

"Oh, you're almost too pretty to look at!" Elizabeth said, hold-ing out her arms to Marie. Marie ran to Elizabeth. As my sisters hugged, I could imagine Elizabeth with little babies of her own. With her patience, she would be a good mother. I felt a sudden swell of love for my sister.

Elizabeth settled Marie into a chair at the table. As she turned back to the stove to get the abelskivvers, a sudden thought shocked me. What if the cold premonition in my heart was for Elizabeth? I didn't know how I could stand to lose my sister. How would I be able to face Peter again if I'd had a warning about Elizabeth and hadn't done anything about it? I clenched my fists and made a firm resolve that I would stick close to Elizabeth and watch over her all day. I'd even quilt with her if I had to.

Ma appeared in the doorway. When she caught sight of me, she said, "Johan, come here, please." Ma glanced at Elizabeth. "You go ahead and feed Marie," she said.

I followed Ma into the back room, throwing a glance over my shoulder. I reassured myself that I would have Elizabeth back in sight in a few minutes. "Ma, what is it?" I asked, my mind in the kitchen.

"Your father has gone to an emergency town meeting," Ma said. "Yesterday Brother John Lowry had an argument with the Indian Jake Arropeen. Arropeen got angry and began to draw an arrow in his bow. Brother Lowry pulled him off his horse, spoke to him sharply, then let him go."

"I wish I'd seen that!" I smiled.

"It's not a funny situation, son," my mother scolded me. "Arropeen went looking for Chief Black Hawk. He found him at the Tooth's house where he was eating dinner after church." I nodded. Chief Black Hawk was a familiar figure in our Sunday meetings. He'd been raised among the white men and had gone to school with the settler's children in our schoolhouse.

"Black Hawk wouldn't see a problem with Brother Lowry defending himself," I said reasonably. "He'd most likely admire him for it."

Ma put a hand on my arm before she said, "There's more to it than that. You know that not very many Indians survived the small pox outbreak last year."

I shrugged. "Lots of settlers died, too."

Ma leaned closer to me. "Yes, but the Indians blame us for bringing the disease in the first place. They claim that we joined forces with Satan in order to afflict them. Not only that, Black Hawk is still smarting from the personal insult when he was caught raiding the Indian Store in Spanish Fork." She extended her arm as though pointing to the very spot. "He was stopped near Payson, and tried to protect his ill-gotten gains with his bow and arrow. One of the brethren was quick to grab a brass bucket that the chief had stolen and toss it over Black Hawk's head." Ma clasped her hands as I tried not to smile. The mental image of the chief with a bucket on his head was awfully amusing. "Not only did he lose all of his plunder, he also lost his dignity," Ma said primly.

"Why are you telling me all this?" I asked, impatient to get back to the kitchen.

"Black Hawk left Brother Tooth's house in a terrible temper. We just don't know what he's up to, so before your father left this morning, he asked that you ride out and bring in all the cattle."

"But we just turned them out to pasture!" I protested.

"You know we need those cows, and we can't take any chances," Ma told me sternly. "The Indians may be out to steal those cattle thinking it will teach us a lesson. We just want to avoid trouble. Get some help because the cows probably won't want to be corralled again after they've tasted fresh grass." I felt torn. I could see the necessity of bringing in the cattle, yet I had to watch over Elizabeth.

"What's wrong, Johan?" Ma said as she searched my face.

"Ma, I have a bad feeling," I said.

"Are you sick?" Ma asked.

"No, not like that. I just have a feeling that something bad is going to happen. It's the same as when Jens died." Ma's jaw dropped as her eyebrows raised in alarm. "I don't know, but maybe it's for Elizabeth," I said soberly.

Ma's hands pressed on either side of her face. "Are you sure?" she asked.

"No, I don't know who or what it is," I said miserably. "It's the way I felt before Dancer broke her leg, too."

Ma nodded tiredly. "All right. Don't worry about Elizabeth. I'll watch her. If anything can be prevented, I'll see to it." Ma wiped her eyes before she gave me a little push. "You go eat, then get those cattle rounded up. Hurry, now."

I didn't feel like eating anymore, but I pushed a couple of abel-skivvers into my mouth before I headed toward the door. Elizabeth stopped me. "Are you going to see Peter?" she asked.

"First thing," I assured her.

"Tell him to stop by later," she said, her face radiant with happiness. "I'm making custard."

"Do I really need to tell him?" I teased her. "It seems that he stops by every day anyhow!"

"But he doesn't always know there will be custard!" she countered, her eyes sparkling with warmth. On impulse, I bent down and gave my sister a quick hug. She returned the hug briefly, then pulled away, a question in her eyes. "What was that for?" she asked.

I shrugged self-consciously. "Just because. Can't I hug my sister if I want to?"

I saddled my horse and headed straight for Peter's house. Shag rose from the front porch to greet me. When I knocked, Peter's mother opened the door. "Peter's in the kitchen with Elmer," she said before I even asked.

Elmer was sitting on Peter's lap, his face pouty and pink from tears. "What's wrong?" I asked.

Elmer turned his face into Peter's shoulder, seemingly embarrassed by the question. "Elmer walks in his sleep," Peter said, wrapping his arms protectively around his little brother. "Last night he got caught in Pa's loom. He hollered so loud that he woke us all up." Peter rolled his eyes above his little brother's head. "Whenever he does that, Pa says the same thing: 'Elmer's up weaving again.' But you don't want to be a weaver, do you, El?" Peter gently rocked Elmer back and forth.

Peter's father Erick was a skilled weaver. Before coming to America he had even woven rugs for the king of Denmark. I couldn't help but grin as I imagined little Elmer tangled in the weaving loom, a reluctant little marionette.

"I came to see if you'd help me bring in the cattle," I said to Peter.

Peter looked at me in surprise. "They were just turned out," he said.

"Indian trouble," I explained. "They might be in a cattle stealing mood."

"I'll go with you," Peter said, standing up and setting Elmer down on a chair where he began to whimper. "It's all right," Peter said, patting his brother on the head. "You can sleep with me tonight if you want to. I'll protect you from the spider web loom!" Peter spread out his fingers on both hands and wiggled them like spider legs before he moved in and tickled Elmer's ribs. Elmer laughed and scooted off the chair.

Sister Ludvigson came into the kitchen. "I'm going out to round up cattle with Johan," Peter told her.

Sister Ludvigson's eyes went wide with worry. "Why would you bring in the cows?" she asked.

"To keep them safe," Peter said lightly.

"Indians!" Sister Ludvigson whispered, her hand pressing on her heart. "They're so dangerous when they're angry. Don't go, Peter, please!"

Peter put his arms around his mother. I turned away, but could still hear him say, "Don't think so much of me, Mother. Some day something might happen to me, and you wouldn't be able to stand it."

A funny little noise came from Sister Ludvigson before she said, "Pete Munk has a pistol. See if you can borrow it."

"Mother, we're just bringing in the cows," Peter protested as he stepped back. "We'll be fine!"

"Please, Peter," his mother said.

Peter relented. "All right. We'll stop by the Munk's. I'll see you for supper."

As we stepped outside, Shag wagged his whole body. "He wants to go with us," I said.

"Yeah, he wants to play cow dog, but he'll only scatter the cows and make it take longer for us to round them up," Peter said as he rumpled Shag's ears. Shag stared adoringly at his master's face. "You've got to stay here, boy." Shag's eyes turned pleading, and a little whine escaped his muzzle. "You don't want to listen to me, do you?" Peter scolded lightly. "This is for your own good," he explained as he pulled a length of rope through the dog's collar and tied a knot. "Elmer will be out to play with you later." Shag tipped his head. I wasn't sure if he was looking forward to playing with Elmer or not. "See you, boy." With a final pat, we left Shag standing at the farthest reach of his rope tether, looking longingly after us.

As we mounted our horses, I said, "Elizabeth says to come over later. She's making custard."

Peter glanced over at me and grinned. "I'll see if I can find the time."

With a couple of other guys to help us, and Pete Munk's pistol in his pocket, Peter and I rode out south of town. The cows looked over their shoulders at us quizzically before swinging their long horns around and moving away from us.

"Oh, no, you don't!" Peter yelled, and pushed his horse into a trot. Suddenly, something flew swiftly through my field of vision and disappeared in front of Peter. He arched his back and fell sideways, landing on the ground with a sickening thud.

"Peter?" I said, staring at the figure of my best friend on the ground while horror chased the cold fear around my heart.

"Indians!" one of the other men shouted. Only then did I recognize the feathered shaft sticking out of Peter's chest. He lay completely still, his unblinking eyes staring at the greening grass pressed against his face. Even as I refused to believe what I was seeing, another arrow found its mark in Peter's body, and still another arrow brushed past in front of my horse.

In blind panic I wheeled and galloped back toward town. The other men scattered like jackrabbits being herded into a catch pen. I headed straight for home, jumping off my horse and racing for the door. Ma's head flew up as I burst into the house. "Johan, what's wrong?" she asked, her brow furrowed.

"They shot Peter!" I yelled. "The Indians killed him!"

"Not Peter!" Ma said, her hands clasping together in a double fist over her heart.

"Noooo!" the wail of protest came from Elizabeth who was sitting in the corner with a needle poised over her embroidery. She dropped the whole thing into her lap without even sticking the needle through the fabric first. She covered her face with her hands and began to cry. It was only then that I realized the cold premonition in my heart was gone. Now all it carried was a big hole filled with pain.

Ma sat by Elizabeth and hugged her for several long minutes. "It's all right, darling, it will be all right," she murmured as Elizabeth continued to cry. When the sobs quieted some, Ma said to me, "Stay with your sister." She threw a shawl over her shoulders. "I'm going to Ludvigsons." I didn't even want to imagine the Ludvigson family when they heard the terrible news. I sat in the chair where my mother had been and held Marie on my lap. I sat by Elizabeth and we cried together.

By the time the news had spread around the settlement, it was too late to do anything about Peter's body. The next morning, Pa asked if I would lead a regiment of militia to the attack site. Even though flanked by armed guards, I felt nervous and twitchy as we approached the place where Peter had fallen. At first I couldn't spot him, but I soon noticed Peter's body a little way off. I felt a flush of anger override my fear when I noticed that the only thing the Indians had left Peter dressed in were his socks. As I rode closer, my indignation rose further when I saw that his body had been purposely thrown face down in a cactus patch. My wrath was shot through with a terrifying chill when I noticed the horrible wound the Indians had inflicted on my dead friend. A long strip of flesh had been cut out of Peter's back along his backbone. The dried blood was spilled down his side in an ugly brown stain. My stomach retched, and I turned my head away as my eyes filled with tears of rage and sorrow.

We wrapped Peter's body up with strips of fabric before we carried him back to town. He could no longer feel the pain of his wounds, but we didn't see any sense in wounding his family further by the sight of the mutilation of their son's body. I hated being there when we carried Peter's body home. I had to be there to show his family that I cared. I don't think anyone but me noticed Shag slip inside the open door, whining softly as we carried our sorrowful burden into the parlor. We laid Peter's body on the couch. The dog stayed by his master's side all night and followed us to the cemetery the next day. After the coffin was buried and the mourners were turning away, Shag climbed onto the mound of soft dirt. He sank down among the sprinkling of wildflowers that had been laid on the grave. He put his head down on his paws, settling in to wait for only he knew what. Every day after that, Shag would head for the cemetery first thing in the morning, wait patiently on the grave all day and return home at dark. This became his regular routine, until one day he was found dead upon his master's grave.

Peter's death signaled the beginning of the Black Hawk War. In spite of my mother's protests, I joined the militia and fought with a vengeance. After three years of fighting, the war eventually wound down to an uneasy truce. This did nothing to heal my sister Elizabeth's heart. She was a shadow of her former self, seeming to have lost her joy for living. She died quietly when she was eighteen, slipping away into the next world where Peter was waiting for her.

Most of the Indians were eventually herded onto reservations, but as the years passed, there always seemed to be some wandering about. I was riding by the Ludvigsons one day when I saw Sister Ludvigson handing some parcels out through the door to a squaw and a brave in a tattered shirt. Three naked brown children flanked the bedraggled couple. I thought I should check to make sure Sister Ludvigson was all right. The smallest child hid his face in his mother's threadbare skirt as I approached. When I dismounted, the Indian family started down the road, the brave throwing a wary glance over his shoulder as I walked up to the door.

"Are you all right?" I asked Sister Ludvigson.

"Of course I am. Why wouldn't I be?"

"I thought maybe those Indians were bothering you."

"Nonsense. They were just hungry."

I looked down the road at the retreating family, my heart hard, and said, "I mean no disrespect to you, but how can you possibly give anything to those savages?"

Sister Ludvigson held up a warning finger. "Now, Johan, they are children of God, just like you and me, only a different color." She searched my face, but must not have been satisfied with what she saw, because she continued. "You think about it; they were here before us, and we came and took their land. What would you do if someone tried to force you out of your home?" I felt some of the rancor leave my heart as I contemplated her words. I truly hadn't thought of it that way before.

"Even though their people killed Peter, God teaches that we must forgive." Sister Ludvigson lifted her chin. "I know I'll see my Peter again. As hard as it is to lose our loved ones, it gives my heart comfort to know that Peter and Elizabeth are together." Sister Ludvigson smiled gently and reached out for my hand. My heart softened at her touch. "We've decided to have Peter and Elizabeth sealed in the temple, and we want you to stand in as proxy for Peter. Will you?"

I stared at Sister Ludvigson, not seeing her face, but instead seeing Peter and Elizabeth together, holding hands, skating around some Celestial ice pond, if they even had ice in heaven. My heart was warm as I answered, "Yes, Sister Ludvigson. I would be honored."

*The personal history of Erick Ludvigson, Sr. tells of his son Peter who was the first man killed during the Black Hawk War in Utah on April 10, 1865. Peter is credited with telling his mother, "Don't think so much of me, Mother. Some day something might happen to me and you wouldn't be able to stand it." After Peter's murder, his sweetheart, Elizabeth Kjar, died on October 16, 1870. The families had the deceased sweethearts sealed together by proxy in the Manti Temple on January 8, 1890. Elizabeth's older brother Johan stood in as proxy for Peter Ludvigson. Her oldest brother Jens had died when Elizabeth was one year old.*

*Rose McIff writes of Elmer Ludvigson, a half brother to Peter Ludvigson. As a young boy, Elmer had the habit of sleepwalking. His father Erick, a weaver by trade, had a loom set up in the house. It was not uncommon for little Elmer to get caught in the strings of the loom during his nightly forays. His father, woken by the commotion, would say in his native Danish, "The little rascal is up weaving again."*

*The same account also tells of Peter Ludvigson's dog, Shag, who guarded his master's dead body all night, then made daily visits to his grave until the day the faithful dog was found dead upon his master's grave.*

*Virginia K. Nielson writes about an incident where Chief Black Hawk was apprehended after stealing supplies from the Indian Farm Store. He was stopped from drawing an arrow in his bow by a brass bucket thrown over his head.   Although other accounts state that the chief was called out of Sacrament Meeting by an angry Jake Arropeen after the brave was pulled roughly off his horse for threatening Brother Lowry with a bow and arrow, Nielson's research and accounts from Edward Tooth's descendents put the location at Edward Tooth's house where Arropeen called Black Hawk away from his dinner and into the Black Hawk War.*

# HOG HEAVEN

Through the window, I saw a woman moving toward the front door of my house. She was tipped sideways at the waist and walked with an odd rolling gait. I knew she couldn't straighten herself, and wondered what it would be like to be trapped in a body that was so crippled. I felt a sudden stab of guilt that was quickly washed with gratitude. The same accident that had crushed my mother's ribs could easily have killed me. I was only three weeks old when a herd of buffalo spooked our wagon team in Wyoming. The panicked oxen broke into a clumsy gallop, throwing my mother and me out of the wagon and onto the ground. Before my father could stop it, a huge wheel bearing the weight of all our earthly possessions rolled over Mother's chest. The same wheel left a dirty trail over the edge of my swaddling clothes. Mother had told me many times during my fifteen years of life how grateful she was that the wagon wheel had struck her instead of me.

Many's the time while growing up that I'd tried to match steps with my crippled mother. It seemed that in order to balance her crooked torso, she had to swing one leg out to step short, then the other leg made a long step, then a short step, then long. She looked the way I imagined a character would from Grimm's Fairy Tales that Mother read to my little brothers at night.

I opened the door for Mother just as she reached it. "Thank you, Eliza!" she said, stepping through the doorway. Her face was pale and she looked tired.

"Are you all right?" I asked as I closed the door.

"Just fine," she answered as she dropped her bundles on the table.

"You seem tired," I insisted. "Your color isn't very good."

Mama plopped wearily into a chair. "Whatever color the good Lord wants to color me is good enough," she replied.

"I thought Pa was with you," I said, throwing a glance at the door.

Without looking up, she said, "He stopped at Mary Ann's."

I put my hands on my hips. "He could have helped you home first, and then gone next door to visit her!" I said hotly.

"The back is made to carry the burden," Mother said firmly.

"It's not even his turn at Mary Ann's," I complained.

"He has his free agency," Mother replied stoutly. "They've only been married a few weeks. He's still getting acquainted."

"They can get acquainted when it's her turn," I said.

Mother looked full into my face before she replied, "I've had him for fourteen years. I mustn't be selfish."

"You've shared him with Anna for five of those years," I reminded her.

"So I had him to myself for nine years," she shrugged her crooked shoulders and started opening her bundles. "It's better than not having a husband at all."

I knew she was referring to my birth father, Joseph Morris, who had abandoned us after we reached Utah. Mother told me that the arid land, Indian troubles, scarcity of food, and bleak future were more than his newly found faith could stand. She had refused to return to England with him, and he refused to settle in a wilderness. He'd found his way to Ogden, Utah and formed the Morrisite Church. As soon as his ex-communication was pronounced, Mother divorced him. Her faith remained as strong as ever.

She counted herself fortunate when Henry Beal married her. Not just any man would take a crippled woman with a baby girl to wife, not knowing if she would be able to bear any more children. Henry's gamble had paid off. He'd been blessed with four vigorous sons from my mother's twisted body, and one two-year-old daughter named Mary Jemima. I was thirteen when Jemima finally came along, and ecstatic to finally have a sister. I hadn't counted on her being stubborn with a voice like a Screech Owl. Jemima's lungs were two sizes too big for her small body.

I helped Mother put her supplies away and start supper. It was Pa's turn to eat at our house, even though he obviously wasn't obligated to spend the hours before the meal in our company. I was still getting used to seeing him only every third night. It used to

# SHIRLEY BAHLMANN

be every other night after he married Anna. Now he had to make time for Mary Ann, too, but he didn't seem to mind.

My brother John came in, his cheeks red from the early summer sun. "Remember to slop the hogs," Mother reminded him.

"I did," John answered, plunging his hands into the washbasin.

"The scrap bucket is still in here," Mother said, "and it's starting to smell."

"I gave them the silage," John said pleadingly. "Besides, Pa's on his way over, so let me give them the scraps tomorrow." His earnest little face was level with Mother's eyes as she regarded him sternly.

She must have read the longing in his eyes to spend time with Pa. "All right, son," she said. John burst into a smile before he rushed outside to escort Pa into the house. All four boys crowded around Pa's legs, making it hard for him to walk.

"Whoa, there," Pa said, patting their heads as he waded through the little bodies to his chair at the table. "Sit down, everyone."

The boys scrambled for their chairs and Jemima stared at Pa from her high chair. "How's my littlest girl today?" Pa said to her over the chatter of the boys trying to talk to him all at once. Jemima answered him with a loud squeal.

Pa looked across the table at me. "How's my biggest girl?" he asked.

My heart warmed at the attention from the only man I could ever remember calling "Pa." He really was charming, cheerful and energetic, with a good sense of humor and a positive outlook on life. "I'm well," I answered with a smile.

After the blessing, Pa gave each of the boys a turn to talk, assuring the ones waiting impatiently that they would each get to have their say. It took up the whole suppertime for my brothers to tell Pa every detail of their lives for the past three days.

When everyone was finished, Mother and I cleaned up while Pa put Jemima on his knee. She stared at him for a moment before she squalled and scrambled to get down. Pa set her on her small feet and she toddled away.

Three-year-old David approached shyly with a cloth ball that Mother had sewn for him. "What have you got there?" Pa asked.

"Ball," David said, and threw it at Pa with all his might. It bounced up off Pa's shoulder before he caught it in mid-air. David giggled and clapped his hands with glee.

"How are things going for you, Mary?" Pa asked my mother as he tossed the ball back. David missed it, and happily chased it across the floor.

"I have to keep after John to finish his chores. George has pretty well taken over the milking, although John spells him off from time to time." Mother wiped her hands on a dishtowel. "Little Henry seems to have quite a head for numbers. He might make a good business manager someday."

"I'll finish up, Mother," I offered. She smiled gratefully at me before she lowered herself into a chair beside Pa.

Pa fielded another wild throw from David, and then said, "Mary Ann sends her regards."

"That's nice of her," Mother said.

"She really is the sweetest person," Pa said with a dreamy smile as he tossed the ball back to David.

"She is very nice," Mother agreed.

"We get along so well, it's as if we knew each other before this life," Pa said fervently. Ma kept smiling at him, but I could see the line that formed between her eyebrows.

"I know it was an answer to prayer for me to marry her," Pa kept on. He covered Mother's hand briefly with his. "Thank you for your consent," he said warmly, unconsciously tipping his head sideways so he could look directly into her eyes. Mother smiled lovingly at him just before David's ball hit Pa in the face, and the tender moment was broken.

Pa stayed for family prayer, then he was gone next door to Mary Ann's. My heart swelled up with resentment, but Mother wouldn't hear me say anything derogatory about Pa.

In the dark of the morning, I heard Ma get up, and then the unmistakable retching of morning sickness. Ma was in a family way. I knew she wouldn't want me to acknowledge her condition until she chose to tell me, so I just lay in the bunk I shared with Jemima and fumed for awhile. If Pa had spent the night, he would know that he was about to add another arrow to his quiver full. If he'd stayed overnight like he ought to have, he would have known Mother wasn't feeling well and would have been more considerate of her. After Mother settled back down alone in her bed, I fell into a restless sleep.

I awakened just before first morning light to the sound of hogs squealing. It was eerie how their squeals sounded so much like Jemima when she was angry. I wondered if John really had given them silage yesterday. Maybe he hadn't given them enough. I thought about rolling him out of bed to go and take care of his chores. Before I could get up, though, I heard Pa's voice from outside call, "Mary, go slop the hogs!"

I sprang up and hurried over to the loft window to look out. The bedroom window of Mary Ann's house was open to the summer morning, and it faced the bedroom where Mother slept. Since there was no one visible in the window opening, I figured that Pa must be calling from the bed he shared with Mary Ann.

John should be taking care of the hogs, not Mother. I resolved to get him up to finish what he was supposed to have done the day before. It wouldn't be easy because John was a sound sleeper. Maybe it would be better if I fed them myself, then made John do one of my chores in exchange.

I was halfway down the stairs when I heard the front door shut. Had John heard Pa's command and gotten up of his own accord to take care of the hogs? It seemed unlikely. I went to Mother's room. Her door was standing open, and her bed was empty. Through the window, I saw her limping toward the hog pen with the scrap bucket in her hand.

I felt indignation well up in my heart. This wasn't right. Yet if I said anything about it when she got back, I could just imagine her answer. "The back is made to carry the burden."

I saw Mother hesitate. Was she going to be sick again? After a moment, she turned and headed toward Mary Ann's house. What was she doing? Was she going to tell Pa that she simply refused, and he could slop the hogs himself? It would serve him right.

I was silently cheering her on as she limped up to the open window. Instead of speaking through it, as I had expected, she pulled back the bucket in her hands and swung it forward. I stared in open-mouthed amazement as the potato peelings, apple cores, and squash rinds went sailing wetly through the window. Yells and squeals of protest sounded from inside the bedroom, but Mother simply turned and walked away, swinging the empty bucket in her lower hand as she tip-walked lightly back to her own house. I never heard Pa complain about his breakfast in bed, and he never missed his turn at our house again.

*Afton C. Greaves tells this story of his great grandparents. In about 1868, Henry Beal was abed with his recently acquired third wife, Mary Ann, when the hogs started to squeal. He shouted out the open window to his first wife, who lived in the house next door, "Mary! Go slop the hogs!" Mary Thorpe Beal, crippled from a wagon accident 15 years earlier that narrowly missed killing her infant daughter, obediently took up the slop bucket and headed toward the hog pen. On the way she was filled with sudden indignation and veered her course toward the bedroom where her husband still lay with Mary Ann. She drew the bucket back, and in one fluid movement, tossed the smelly contents onto the bed.*

*Her first husband, Joseph Morris, moved to Ogden, Utah, left the church, and formed his own sect called the Morrisites.*

# FIDDLESTICKS

I was scrubbing out the last pan from dinner when I heard my little sister Raphine shout delightedly, "They're here! They're here!" Raphine was only eight years old and couldn't possibly understand all the work that now lay before me. I groaned and my shoulders slumped in fatigue. When I was Raphine's age, I had looked forward to our roadhouse visitors, too, but lately I only saw them as so much more work. I had been cooking and cleaning all day, and I was not looking forward to feeding a wagonload of young men passing through on their assignment to work on the St. George Temple. Even though they were expected, I had hoped they would have broken a wheel or tipped their wagon off the road. I didn't want anything deadly, just a minor inconvenience that would prevent them from getting here until tomorrow, after I'd had a good night's sleep.

I did a mental tally of what I would need to do now before I could go to bed. At twenty years old, I was the eldest in a family of nine children, and being a girl made me Ma's right hand. She especially needed me because we let out rooms to travelers.

Pa loved running the roadhouse. He eagerly greeted visitors, talking easily about where they'd been and where they were going, catching up on news from far away places. With five daughters, he didn't even need to hire help for cooking, washing or making up the rooms. My eighteen-year-old brother Augustinas helped in the stables and worked our small farm with Pa. The youngest three in our family were boys six, four, and two years old. If that weren't enough, Ma had just confided in me that she was going to have another baby.

I turned the pan that I had just finished washing right side up and began filling it with water. Seventeen-year-old Heddy came into the kitchen. "Mina, Mama says to start supper," she told me.

"I already have," I said as I plunked the pan of water on top of the wood stove. "Heddy, get some biscuit dough mixed, please."

"Raphine, I need some more firewood," I told my youngest sister as I pulled open the kindling door on the stove and pushed in a few sticks.

"It's not my turn," Raphine whined. "I got the wood for dinner!"

"It's the turn of whoever's here when I need it," I said firmly.

"But, Mina!" Raphine protested.

"Would you rather milk the cow?" I asked her sternly. "That needs to be done, too."

"No, I'll get the wood," Raphine huffed as she swept out of the kitchen.

With my sisters' help, I finished the dinner preparations and even managed to get the cow milked. Pa came in to check on our progress. "It's ready! Good," Pa said. "I'll call the men in to eat. They're famished!"

I began carrying food to the table. The men descended on the food like crows on a cornfield, and I worried if there would be enough. After the blessing was said, I didn't even sit down. There were empty plates to shuttle off to the kitchen and full plates to bring back. As I slid a fresh plate of bread onto the table in between two men, I accidentally bumped one of them.

"Sorry," I said, glancing quickly at him in apology.

I noticed his handsome dark blonde hair just before his deep gray-blue eyes caught mine and held them. Instead of diving into the plate of fresh bread, his eyes lingered. I felt as though I was looking into the heart of deep water, calm on the surface but embroiled with deep secrets of an unseen world within.

"No, I'm the one who's sorry," he said.

"What for? It wasn't your fault," I said.

"It's my fault that I haven't thanked you for dinner."

My breath caught. "You're welcome," I answered softly.

"More milk, Mina," Pa called from the head of the table. I tore my eyes away and hurried to do Pa's bidding.

When everyone was finally satisfied, my sisters and I began clearing the table. "This seems like a time for celebration," Pa said as I picked up his plate. "But our local fiddler broke his arm last week. We don't have any music."

"Hans," someone called out. Several other young men echoed the name. "Hans." "Ask Hans." "Hans can play."

"Hans?" Pa asked.

The dark blonde man stood and gave Pa a little wave even as his eyes found mine. My heart seemed to push out painfully against my chest, straining toward the young man. "I am Hans," he said as though he was speaking to Pa, but I knew he was introducing himself to me.

"Can you fiddle?"

Hans tipped his head slightly from side to side. "A little," he answered.

"Would you play for us tonight?"

Hans smiled, his eyes still on me. "Yes, I would like to," he answered. I smiled at him then, and he raised one corner of his mouth teasingly. The expression on his face seemed to charge across the room and spear my heart, making me feel curiously light-headed.

With Hans on my mind, cleaning up the meal took no time at all. Before I knew it, I was seated in the large room that Pa had built for the entertainment of our guests. The hardwood floor was polished to the perfect finish for dancing. Hans pulled his fiddle from its battered black case and plinked the strings, twisting the knobs on the neck until he was satisfied with the sound that came forth. Then he began a tune so lively that all my fatigue vanished. A young man with a face as long as a horse's asked me to dance and I eagerly accepted. All of my sisters were already up and dancing, even Raphine, who giggled at all the attention she was getting.

There was no resting for my sisters or me since the men out-numbered the women at this gathering. As I danced, I couldn't help stealing glances at Hans. He stood alone at the side of the big room, working his bow into a blur across the fiddle strings, his eyes disconcertingly fastened on me.

After awhile, Pa called for a break and asked me to get the cake from the kitchen. He sent all my sisters in to help me while Ma put the little boys to bed. We served cake all around. I purposely saved the last plate for Hans. Besides the cake, I handed him a glass of cold buttermilk. He smiled gratefully and drained half of it at once.

"Please sit by me," he invited. He didn't have to ask me twice.

I sat down and Hans took a bite of cake. "You're very good," I said.

"So's this cake," he replied. He turned his heart-stopping blue eyes on me. "Did you make it?"

"Yes, probably," I answered.

"You don't know?" he said.

"I do a lot of the cooking, but Heddy helps, too. It's just that all the days run together, and I can't really remember exactly what I do when." I shrugged. "I just do whatever needs to be done."

"There must be a lot to do around here," he said. I nodded. His words were a reminder that the smart thing to do would be to go to bed right now because I'd need to get up early enough to fix breakfast for all our visitors.

Hans broke into my thoughts. "Do you like it here?"

I turned startled eyes to him. "I suppose so." I'd never really thought about it before. Here was my family and the only life I'd ever known.

"Have you traveled?" he asked.

"No," I said. "It's next to impossible to get someone to take over and run this place. Sometimes Ma and Pa go, then Augustinus and I take care of everything until they get back."

"Have you ever wanted to go somewhere else?"

"No, not particularly." I thought of all that was expected of me, and met Hans' gaze guiltily. "Well, not until lately," I admitted. Hans stared at me for a few moments until I began to wonder what was on his mind. "You didn't get any cake," he said, picking up a piece with his fork. "Have some."

I opened my mouth to protest and Hans slid the fork in. I smiled shyly and chewed the bite of sweet cake, letting myself feel how good it was to have someone taking care of me and making sure I got some good things in life.

I didn't go to bed early. I stayed until Hans was all fiddled out, and even then, I went up to my room reluctantly, glancing back at Hans to see him watching me go, his breathing coming hard as beads of sweat ran down the sides of his face. The intensity of his stare sent shivers up my back. I didn't fall asleep easily. Knowing that Hans was in the same house as me made me feel warm and restless.

In spite of my brief sleep, I was instantly awake just as the sky was turning an early morning gray. None of my sisters so much as moved a little finger as I hurried out of bed and made my way downstairs. I milked the cow first thing, then carried the milk to the cellar to strain it and set it out in pans to cool. As I carried the bucket up the cellar steps toward the kitchen, I was startled to see Pa standing at the top of the stairs.

"Mina, I need to talk to you," he said, his stern face showing none of the good cheer he'd displayed for his guests last night.

"What's wrong?" I asked as he stepped back to let me into the kitchen.

"I don't quite know how to say this," Pa said as he lowered himself into a chair.

"Just say it," I urged, sitting down beside him and setting the bucket on the floor.

Pa scratched his head. "Do you remember the fiddler from last night? The one they called Hans?"

"Yes, of course," I said. My heart hammered alarmingly at the mention of his name. Had Hans gone? Was he hurt? I leaned forward to the edge of my chair as though that would urge Pa to speak more quickly.

"Well, last night I asked him if he would play for the party I had planned for tonight."

I raised my eyebrows. "You didn't cancel it?"

Pa looked over at me sheepishly. "No. After Brother Alder broke his arm, I kept hoping that a miracle would occur." His face brightened. "And it has! The good Lord sent Hans so that we could still have the dance."

"Is that all you wanted to tell me?" I asked, puzzled.

Pa's face became grave again. I tensed, steeling my heart for what he might say. "It's not so easy," he said. "I asked Hans to play for tonight, but he said he felt he had an obligation to follow the Lord's call and go on to the St. George Temple. I tried to reason with him, that one more day wouldn't delay the Lord's work. After some coaxing, he finally stated the terms by which he would agree to stay on for one more night."

Pa was silent for so long, I had to urge him to continue. "What are the terms?" I asked.

Pa looked solemnly into my eyes. "He asked for your hand in marriage."

I gripped the sides of my chair so I wouldn't fall off as a warm flush weakened my bones and crept up into my face. "He wants to marry me?" I whispered.

"He said that's the only thing that would make him stay."

A curious excitement radiated from my heart and made my limbs tingle. "He wants to marry me," I repeated.

"It was an impertinent thing to ask," Pa said, shaking his head at the brazenness of it. "I'll tell him he'd just better get on the wagon with the rest of the fellows."

"But I want to," I said.

"You want to tell him?" Pa raised his eyebrows at me in surprise.

"No. I want to marry him." The image of Hans' intense gray-blue eyes with depth that would take a lifetime to fathom came forcefully to mind. I could again taste the piece of sweet cake that he fed to me. I suddenly realized I was ready for change. I wanted adventure in my life, and I wanted to go on that adventure with Hans.

"Are you sure?" Pa asked me.

"Yes."

Pa looked somewhat chagrined. "When Hans first stated his terms, I was ready to send him packing. But your mother said I had to tell you first." Pa reached his hand over to briefly cover mine. "It appears that mother knew best. We'll miss you, dear."

I leaned over to hug my father. Just then Raphine came pattering into the kitchen. "Mama says to get breakfast going," she said. She tipped her head as Pa and I pulled apart. "What's the matter?" she asked.

"Your sister is getting married," Pa said gruffly.

Raphine's eyes went wide. "Which one?" she asked. Pa and I both burst out laughing.

When Hans came to breakfast, his eyes lit up in greeting when he saw me. The process of getting the other fellows off on the wagon to continue their journey kept us so busy that we didn't have a chance to talk alone. The eyes that caught mine at dinnertime were dark and smoldering with intensity. I knew Pa had told Hans my decision, since he hadn't gotten on the wagon with the rest of the men. Being the object of such ardent attention made me feel conspicuous, and I kept myself in the kitchen all afternoon making cake and cookies for the evening's festivities. I desperately wanted to be with Hans, but I felt unexpectedly shy. I wasn't sure what to say to him.

Guests began arriving for the party, but I didn't let myself come out of the kitchen until I heard the fiddle start playing. I didn't need to fill in as a partner for anyone this time, because there was a more balanced mix of men and women. I brought out the refreshments and set them on the sideboard that Pa had set up. I studiously avoided looking at Hans. When all was settled, I asked my sisters Heddy and Caroline to keep an eye on replenishing the food. Then I cut a piece of cake, set it on a plate with a single fork, and carried it to the chair closest to Hans. I sat down before I glanced up at him. His eyes crinkled in amusement when he recognized what I was holding on my lap. As I took in his mischievous expression, all my nervousness melted away. A flash of certainty coursed through me with all the heat and force of a lightning bolt. I knew from a place deep within my soul that Hans was the man I wanted to marry, to be with forever and ever.

Eventually Hans stopped fiddling and sat in a chair beside me. I handed him the plate and began to rise. Alarmed, he put a restraining hand on my arm. "Where are you going?" he asked.

"To get you something to drink."

Hans stared into my eyes. "Nothing will satisfy me like being with you," he said. "I've been starving for you all day. Please stay with me."

"All right," I answered. We again shared the cake, and when Raphine came to take the plate, I asked her for some milk.

"There, now, that worked out just fine, didn't it?" Hans said cheerily. I nodded. "Do you know what else could work out just fine?" he asked, leaning in close to me and speaking softly.

"What?" I leaned toward him in order to hear better. We were so close that I could feel his hair against my forehead like a gentle kiss.

"You marrying me tonight."

A thrill ran through me. "Tonight?" I asked.

"Yes. Mina, will you marry me tonight?" The thought flashed through my head that Hans would be leaving for St. George in the morning. If I didn't marry him now, I would be left behind, cooking, washing, cleaning, and tending children as I waited for Hans to come back and claim me someday.

"Yes," I said firmly.

"Mina, darling!" Hans said, lifting my hand to his mouth for a kiss that sent a river of warmth up my arm and straight to my heart. He stood up and hurried away to speak to my father. Pa's eyebrows shot up before he shifted his gaze to look past Hans at me. I nodded my head. Pa looked at Hans again, then smiled a rueful little smile. He turned and said something to Ma before he headed out the door. Hans hurried over to me and took up his fiddle with a flourish. "Your father's gone to get the bishop," he announced. "Let's celebrate!"

My mother followed at a more sedate pace and plopped down in Hans' vacant seat with my two-year-old brother sagging sleepily in her arms. "Mina, are you happy?" she asked, a look of gentle concern on her face.

Han's fiddle was playing, making my heart skip merrily along with the tune. I thought of my life with him, and knew that whatever the trials, whatever the struggles we would face together, there would always be Hans and his music to take the weariness out of life. "Yes, I am," I replied. "I'm as happy as," I paused to think, trying to come up with just the right description so that Ma would understand. "I'm as happy as a fiddler's wife."

*According to Talula Nelson's family story, Hans Peter Hansen stopped at the Nelson's place in Richfield, Utah in 1875 with a group of young men who were on their way to work on the St. George Temple. Hans played his fiddle for the company's entertainment, and made such an impression that Brother Nelson asked him to stay to provide music for a party he had planned for the next night. Hans was reluctant, feeling a need to continue on his journey and begin his temple building assignment. Hans eventually admitted that it would be worth his while to fiddle if he could marry Brother Nelson's daughter Mina. With Mina's consent, the agreement was made. The next night, on impulse, they got the bishop out of bed and were married at midnight, then celebrated by dancing until dawn.*

# CINDERELLA CATHERINE

Penelope's cold, prickly laugh grated across my ears like a cockleburr. "Oh, Peter, you're so funny!" she cackled. My oldest brother Peter murmured a reply, but his voice was so deep and mellow that I couldn't make out the words.

I shifted my weight from one foot to the other as I waited impatiently, out of sight in the hall, while Peter continued to bid goodbye to his sweetheart. I needed to pass through the foyer to the parlor where I was supposed to be dusting, but I didn't want to go anywhere near Penelope.

When I'd first seen her, I had stared in a manner that my mother would have called rude, but I couldn't help myself. I was an awkward ten-year-old, and Penelope's honeyed hair curled most becomingly in little ringlets next to her cheeks while the rest of her long tresses were pinned up in glimmering swirls on the back of her head. I secretly wondered if she was a real princess. I was also convinced that because Peter and Penelope's names sounded so good together, they were meant for each other.

I soon realized that there was more to romance than names that started with the same letter. Penelope's beauty gradually faded as I noticed how much stock she put in herself. She became downright ugly a month after my eleventh birthday. She was tatting some lace while she waited for Peter in the parlor.

I was tending my little brother Roy in the kitchen. He was nearly two years old, and a very busy boy. I was helping to peel apples for cobbler when Roy toddled away from me and down the hall. I followed his progress with my eyes until I saw him disappear into the parlor. I rubbed my hands on my apron as I hurried to retrieve him. I got to the parlor doorway just in time to see Roy put his hands out toward Penelope's knees for balance so he could grin up at her angel-like beauty. Penelope jerked her knees away at the last moment, wearing an expression of disgust that contorted her perfect features into a face I didn't recognize. Roy lost his balance and fell on his soft, round tummy, his stunned expression twisting itself into a howl of disappointment and betrayal. I strode into the room and scooped up my brother, hastening him out as

Penelope's words trailed after me. "Oh, dear, is he all right? The poor little boy tripped on the rug, and I couldn't catch him in time."

I didn't know how to tell Peter what had happened without sounding like a Harpy. It would be Penelope's word against mine, and I didn't have to think very hard to decide who he would believe.

"I really have to go, Petie, it's my only chance," Penelope's voice from the foyer was probably meant to be playful but sounded whiny.

Mama passed me in the hall, her arms piled with sheets and her mouth set in a straight line. She didn't smile when she saw me. That was a bad sign. "Have you done your dusting?" she asked brusquely. I knew she wasn't thrilled about Peter's engagement to Penelope, but it wasn't my fault.

"Almost," I answered in a small voice. I really didn't want to be scolded. It was my next-to-least favorite thing to happen to me. Having Penelope for a sister-in-law was my least favorite.

Before Mama could say more than, "Lilly!" in a voice that signaled she'd reached the end of her patience, someone spoke up from behind us. "I'll help her. I'm done in the kitchen anyway."

My heart lifted at the familiar voice, which sounded as though a chuckle could break to the surface at any moment. Mama and I both turned to see Catherine walking toward us. She was flapping her wet apron skirt, her gray eyes lit with good humor.

Mama's voice calmed. The scolding was forgotten. "Thank you, Catherine." Then she turned to me and said pointedly, "What do you say, Lilly?"

"Thank you, Ma'am," I grinned at Catherine as I dipped an exaggerated curtsy.

"Cheeky," Catherine said in mock severity as she plunked one hand on her hip and tilted her nose in the air. I giggled and Mama even let herself crack a smile.

"Enough of your sass," Mama said to me, unable to wipe the amusement clear off her face.

"I'll teach her some manners, Sister Greaves," Catherine said firmly as she took hold of my shoulder and turned me toward the foyer. I wasn't the least bit cowed. Catherine's lesson would be most welcome, as it would probably include ridiculous instruction such as holding out your little pinkie finger as you wielded the duster, and running your nose along the mantel, checking for sneezes to make sure you got all the dust.

As I stepped into the foyer, Penelope's blue eyes cut over to me with accusation seated in their cold depths. I supposed she was annoyed at being interrupted by a mere child and a servant girl. With her eyes on me, her hands slid up onto my brother's shoulders, slow and sinuous, like two snakes meeting for a deadly embrace behind his neck.

Peter looked down at me, and then glanced up at Catherine. "Is Lilly in trouble again?" he asked lightly.

"Oh, absolutely," Catherine replied. "The Pinkerton detectives are canvassing the house this afternoon to search for illegal dust. Lilly has a whole stash of it in the parlor."

Peter gave a little laugh. "Keep her on the straight and narrow," he said.

"I'll do my best to keep her out of jail," Catherine replied as her hand propelled me through enemy territory and into the safety of the ornate parlor. Mama had filled it with carved furniture and lamps with dangling crystals that sparkled like laughter when tickled by a feather duster.

"But it's so cold out there!" Penelope cackled from the foyer.

"I'll keep you warm," Peter said just before I heard the sound of the front door open. Penelope's answering titter was blessedly silenced when the door closed.

As Catherine cheerfully pitched in with the cleaning, I thanked my lucky stars for the day she had agreed to come help my mother with housework. Catherine was a Mortensen, part of a good family that was not very well off financially. Mama had been overwhelmed with the housekeeping, and Catherine was a hard worker, so it was a good arrangement for everyone. Especially me.

When we finished cleaning, we found Mama in the kitchen trying to write with Roy in her lap. His chubby little hand was busy grabbing at the pen. Mama's hand was busy trying to keep it away from him.

"Are you the scribe?" Catherine asked, pulling Roy away from Mama and sitting him in the circle of her arms so that he faced her. "Who can read your writing anyway? Is it two-year-old secret code so only two-year-olds can read it?"

"I two," Roy declared proudly, holding up his pudgy hand with all the fingers sticking up.

"Yes, you're two, too cute and too smart!" Catherine declared, spinning around in a circle, making Roy laugh and grab hold of her bodice with both hands so he wouldn't fall backwards.

When Catherine stopped moving her feet, she stood and swayed side to side. "Oooo, Roy, you made me dizzy!" she laughed.

"Catherine," Mama said.

Catherine moved her eyes from Roy's laughing face to Mama's serious one. "Yes?" she answered.

"I've decided to send you to a finishing school in Salt Lake City."

I stared at Mama in stunned disbelief. Why would she want to send Catherine away? She couldn't! Catherine already knew how to finish things. My mind grasped for something, anything to come to Catherine's defense. "We finished the dusting," I said helpfully, emphasizing the "finish."

"That's fine, Lilly," Mama replied absently before she again spoke to Catherine. "You're scheduled to leave next week."

Catherine's eyes were as startled as if she'd just stepped on broken glass. "But, Sister Greaves..." Catherine began.

Mama held up her hand and Catherine obediently stopped speaking. "I want to do this, Catherine. Please let me. I don't want to hear any protests." Mama smiled hopefully. "Humor me."

Catherine's warm gray eyes studied my mother briefly over the top of Roy's head. She gave a slow nod just before Roy patted her cheek softly. "Again!" he burbled, grabbing Catherine's dress in his hands just in time to keep from tipping backwards as she spun in a dizzying circle.

After supper, Catherine and I were alone in the kitchen washing dishes. "Catherine, do you really want to go to finishing school?" I asked. I was hoping to hear her declare her utter distaste at the idea of leaving, that she would never leave me and Roy.

Instead, Catherine tipped her head to the side as she plunged her hands into the dirty dishpan. "I hardly know what to think," she said. Her eyes slid to the window above the sink and stayed there, gazing out as she spoke. "I think it would be grand to be a fine lady," she said dreamily. I couldn't figure out what that had to do with anything, but I remained silent. Catherine looked sideways at me and raised her eyebrows. "Besides, if I knew all the rules of etiquette, I could be a greater help to your mother," she said. Keen disappointment coursed through me, and I shut down my heart and didn't speak any more of the matter. It seemed too soon when Catherine packed her bags and left.

There was a heavy snowfall the day after the train swallowed Catherine and belched its way toward Salt Lake City. The cold carried over to the house, which seemed awfully empty without Catherine. Thankfully, it was also free of Penelope. She had gone on a train with her mother, headed for the eastern states to help her sister who'd just had twin babies. Poor babies, I thought, and refused to feel bad.

I caught myself more than once expecting Catherine to walk through the doorway at any moment, only to remember with a sinking heart that she was far away in Salt Lake City.

One day, Mama said, "Lilly, I know you miss Catherine, but please realize this is a wonderful opportunity for her."

"Why?" I asked. "Catherine already knows how to finish things. She finished every job you ever gave her."

Mama gave me a puzzled look, then smiled and shook her head. "A finishing school doesn't teach you how to finish chores," she said gently. "It's for the finishing touches of social grace and good manners. It finishes social training, so to speak."

Her explanation left me feeling small, stupid, and defensive. "I would rather socialize with Catherine than some other young ladies I know," I said darkly.

To my surprise, Mama didn't scold, but nodded thoughtfully. "She is a pleasant girl," Mama agreed. "And she'll be more marriageable with the proper training."

I stared at Mama. "Married?" I blurted. "If she gets married, she'll move away! Why do you want Catherine to move away? I want her to stay here!"

Mama pulled her eyebrows down and looked at me. "Things change, Lilly. Nothing stays the same. People grow up, some get married, some move away." She shrugged. "People die, and people are born." Mama rested her hand lightly on her tummy. I hadn't noticed until just this minute that her stomach was round and pushed against the fabric of her skirt.

I looked up into Mama's smiling face. "Another baby?" I asked. She nodded. "Oh, I hope it's a girl!" I said fervently.

"That's up to Heavenly Father," Mama said. "He'll send us whoever we're supposed to have."

"I'm going to pray for a girl," I said.

"It's a little late for that," Mama answered. I didn't say anything, but secretly held on to my resolve to pray for a little sister. I believed in a God of miracles.

Penelope returned a few weeks after Christmas. Thankfully, she didn't come to the house as often, but now Peter was gone more than he used to be. He had more time on his hands since harvest was over and the fields were covered in thick, white blankets of snow for the winter. He and Penelope went out for sleigh rides, to dances, and watched traveling minstrel shows.

Catherine wrote to me often. I spent a lot of the slow winter days writing return letters describing Roy's antics and the new words he was learning, as well as Mama's progressively growing belly and Peter's social forays.

I vividly remember the day of the first thaw. Roy took a fever and was put to bed. At first I thought he would be over it in no time. He had such energy that I couldn't imagine him lying still for very long. Yet as the days passed, his fever got worse, and his breathing more shallow. I didn't write much to Catherine anymore. I spent my time sitting beside Roy when Mama had to lie down. She said her back hurt from the baby. I couldn't understand how her back could hurt from having a big tummy, but it wasn't the time to question her about it. I read stories to Roy or sponged his brow with cool water. When he was awake, he liked me to sing "Come, Come, Ye Saints" as long as I marched around the room and pantomimed the actions of the words I was singing. I would pretend to chop wood for "toil nor labor" and when I sang "fear" I'd duck down beside his bed and peek over the edge at him as though he was a fearsome creature. He would laugh shallowly, ending with a hoarse cough. His eyes would shine, and he would say, "Again, Lilly, again," until he was too exhausted to keep his eyes open.

Pa came in to check on his little boy often. If Roy was asleep, Pa would ask me how he was doing. I would tell him all I could, feeling safe while Pa was there. If Roy was awake, he'd stretch his little arms out to Pa and Pa would sit and rock with him.

As spring turned the outdoors into a child's fresh, green playground, Roy seemed to grow smaller and weaker in his dark little room. He slept more and for longer periods, his mouth open as the breath rasped in and out, his eyebrows pinched together even in sleep as he worked his lungs to get the air he needed.

Mama sat in a chair by the bedside when Pa and Peter brought in consecrated oil to give Roy a blessing. Roy was asleep and didn't move so much as an eyelid when Peter leaned over and anointed him. Both men put their hands on his head and Pa spoke the words of the blessing. I remember him asking that the Lord's will be done. Mama was silently weeping when the blessing ended. Pa put his arm around her and turned her out of the room, murmuring softly to her.

Peter sat on the edge of our baby brother's bed. The room was darkened as much by sorrow as by the curtains that were drawn across the windows. When Peter picked up Roy's small hand, Roy rolled toward Peter and snuggled into his side with a shallow little sigh. Peter didn't even try to stop the tears that rolled down his face. "Oh, Roy," he said in an anguished whisper. I slipped out the door unnoticed and went to my own room to cry.

When I had cried all I was able, I took up paper and pen. "Dear Catherine," I wrote. "Pa gave Roy a blessing, but he didn't say for Roy to be healed. He just said the Lord's will be done. Heavenly Father has to heal Roy. He is suffering so, poor boy. When are you coming back? Are you finished yet? Love from Lilly."

Peter didn't go out much anymore. He did what he had to in order to prepare the fields for planting, but he cut back his social outings. Penelope came to the house a time or two, but she wouldn't go in the sick room and soon tired of trying to coax Peter out. I was relieved when she stopped coming to our house altogether.

I was alone with Roy when he died. The silence that followed his last rasping breath screamed out like an alarm. I scooped up Roy's thin little body and shook it. "Breathe!" I commanded my little brother. "C'mon, Roy, you've got to breathe!" I stopped shaking and stared into Roy's face, which had relaxed into an unearthly calm. The constant frown of pain was gone from his brow. My baby brother's face was smooth and relaxed. I gradually realized that Roy was finally free. I pulled his little body close to my heart. He didn't move, or snuggle in, or even wiggle to get away. He was gone.

Pa opened the door. "Lilly?" he asked. "Are you all right? I could only shake my head. My tears were wetting Roy's hair as I rested my cheek on it. Pa walked slowly over to us and bent down, wrapping his big arms around both Roy and me. Pa and I cried while Roy lay still against my aching breast.

The next day when Pa got back from making funeral arrangements, he brought me a letter from Catherine. "Lilly, I am worried about little Roy. I pray for him morning and night. I miss you so much, but never fear! I will be finished next month and am coming to help your mother when she has the baby. I can't wait to see you and Roy and the rest of the family. Give Roy a big hug for me and tell him I'll see him soon. All my love, Catherine."

Pa took care of sending Catherine a telegram with news of Roy's death. It had only been two months since he took sick, but felt like a lot longer. Mama cried all the way through the funeral. I couldn't sing "Come, Come Ye Saints" at the graveside because my throat closed up every time I opened my mouth, so I just gave up and cried. Penelope was there, sitting beside Peter, holding onto his arm like an ivy vine twined around a trellis. She occasionally dabbed at her dry eyes with a lacy handkerchief.

Roy was finally laid to rest, his coffin so small it seemed impossible to contain the mischief and joy that Roy had exuded from his small body during his short life. Pa didn't make it all the way through the dedication prayer without his voice breaking. He stood silent for so long, that I opened my eyes and peeked at him. Bishop Hollis moved in beside him and put his arm around Pa's shaking shoulders. The touch of the clergyman seemed to help Pa collect himself enough to finish the prayer in a halting voice.

The house seemed dark and quiet without Roy. Mama took to her bed, from sorrow more than the huge size of her belly. The doctor worried about the baby being healthy because of Mama's state of mind. Pa and Peter gave Mama a blessing, using the same vial of oil they had used on Roy.

When Mama awoke the next morning, I could hear her talking to Pa from the other side of the bedroom door. Her voice was light and animated. She actually sounded happy.

I knocked timidly on the door. "Come in!" Mama sang out.

I opened the door softly and stepped inside, pushing the door closed with my back. "Come closer, Lilly dear," Mama said, holding out her arms to me, a beautific smile on her face. I hadn't seen Mama smile in so long, she looked like a stranger. I glanced over at Pa. He was sitting on the side of the bed, staring at me through wet eyes. Was Mama losing her mind? I'd heard about an asylum in Provo where crazy people went. Sometimes people went crazy with grief. A cold fear clutched at my heart. I didn't want Mama to be crazy. I just wanted her to be my normal everyday Mama who made me do my chores and told me what a pretty young lady I was becoming.

Before I could decide if I wanted to step into this crazy lady's arms, a knock sounded. Peter put his head around the door. "Where is everybody?" he asked.

"We're all in here," Mama called, "And now I can tell both of you at once. Roy's all right!"

My heart lurched. "He's not dead?" I asked incredulously.

"Of course he's dead," Peter said tightly. "What are you talking about, Mother?" he said slowly. His face was creased with worry.

"Roy's happy now," Mama said, stretching her arms beseechingly toward us. "He can run and play. He doesn't want us to grieve any more. He especially wants us to be happy for the sake of your baby sister."

I glanced down to see if I had missed something. Mama's belly was still as big and round as when she had gone to bed the night before. "How do you know it's a girl?" I asked.

"Roy told me," Mama said. My heart drooped. Mama was going crazy. Roy couldn't tell her anything. He was dead.

"He couldn't," I said flatly.

"I saw Roy last night while I was asleep," Mama said.

"So you dreamed about Roy," said Peter.

"It was more than a dream," Mama insisted. "I know I was blessed to see my little boy. He looked so happy, I just can't be sad for him anymore."

I felt a little tingle run along the back of my neck. I really wanted to believe everything Mama was saying.

There was a ghost of a smile on Pa's face. "Did you see him, too?" Peter asked pointedly.

Pa shook his head. "No," he said. "But I believe your mother. The spirit world is closer than we think." With Pa's reassurance, I was beginning to feel comforted to hear that Roy was truly happy now, but I felt a little piqued that Roy had not favored me with a visit. After all, I had spent the most time taking care of him at the very end of his life. Yet my parent's joy was contagious, and I soon forgave Roy for not visiting me in the night. Maybe he thought I would be scared, and he was much too tender hearted to ever want to scare me. Or maybe he just couldn't wake me up.

With our family renewed by the message of love and hope from Roy, the days flew by until finally it was the morning that Catherine was coming in on the train. I was so excited I couldn't eat breakfast.

"Son, I need you to go pick up Catherine from the station," Pa said.

Peter pulled his head up with a start. "But I had other plans," he complained. I was pretty sure his other plans were Penelope.

"It won't take you long," Pa assured him. "I've got someone coming to see me about a horse, and I need to talk to him. We can't leave Catherine stranded at the station. Now take Lilly and go."

Peter threw his napkin down on the table without finishing his food. He pushed back in his chair and grumbled, "The train had better not be late."

I skipped along beside him as we went out to get the buggy. It took Peter forever to hitch up the horse, even though I helped him all I could. I was disappointed that we arrived at the station ahead of the train, but not as disappointed as Peter. We climbed down from the wagon and Peter paced while I kept craning my neck every few seconds to look as far along the rails as I could for any sign of the train. After enduring Peter's grumbling, it was with relief that I finally spotted the smudge of black from the train's smokestack in the distance. I caught myself jumping up and down and made myself stop. I wanted to show Catherine that I was a regular young lady now. I hoped for Peter's sake that Catherine would be one of the first ones off the train.

The train huffed slowly into the station, shushing to a stop as people called greetings from the ground to the passengers in the windows. People trickled off the train like kernels of wheat escaping from the corner of a gunnysack. I scanned the faces for Catherine, but couldn't spot her. I noticed a man with the widest handlebar moustache I had ever seen, a young mother with three children clinging to her skirts, and a refined lady in a striking red plumed hat. I only gave them a cursory glance, because I wasn't interested in anyone but Catherine. I sought the faces of all the young ladies dressed in gray and brown, but none of them was Catherine. Had she changed her mind? My heart chilled at the sudden thought that maybe she wasn't coming because Roy was dead.

I took Peter's hand hoping that it would calm my fears. "Where is she?" I whispered. When Peter didn't answer, I looked up at him and caught him staring at the girl in red. She was walking toward us with a suitcase in each hand. I thought she looked ridiculous with her flamboyant hat dipped over half her face, and couldn't imagine how she could even see to walk. When Peter took a step toward her, I angrily tugged his arm. This was no time for chivalry. We were here to find Catherine, not for him to offer his help to some flashy stranger.

My tug was ineffective, and Peter kept going until he was facing the lady in red. Her dress had one of those new bustles on the back, and a swath of fabric across the front at hip level that was tucked and gathered at the sides like a little apron. The lady had to stop in order to keep from bumping into my brother. "Excuse me, ma'am, could I help you with your cases?" Peter asked, as smooth as honey taffy.

The lady tipped her head up and said, "Why, yes, Peter, that would be splendid."

Peter completely lost his composure, opening his eyes wide to add to the dumbest look I'd ever seen on his face. "Catherine?" he asked, his eyebrows raised nearly to his hairline.

Catherine laughed. "I'm so pleased you haven't forgotten about me in my absence," she said. I stood staring at the lady who used to be my friend. She looked different and she talked different. I didn't like the way she was finished at all. I liked her better before.

Catherine turned and saw me standing uncertainly in my best dress, one brown ringlet twisting around and around my finger. "Lilly!" she cried, and knelt in a most unladylike fashion, her arms open wide. I melted into her embrace, relieved that she was still the same Catherine inside.

Catherine and I stood arm in arm and faced Peter. "Is your offer to help me with my cases still good?" Catherine said with a coy smile.

Peter almost tripped over his own feet in his haste to pick up Catherine's luggage. He led the way to the buggy while we followed behind, giggling and talking about all that had happened while we were apart. I realized that Catherine was the same, but better somehow. She was more sure of herself, and more refined, like a real lady. But she was still sweet and good inside. It was as though she had left as a cinnamon roll and come back with extra frosting.

110

Catherine sat in the front seat next to Peter and I sat in back with the cases and eavesdropped on their conversation. Peter was very attentive, leaning toward Catherine in order to hear every word she said. My parents greeted Catherine warmly, and we were so entertained by her stories of finishing school that before I knew it, it was the end of the day. I suddenly realized that Peter had completely neglected his other plans.

Mama wasn't the least bit surprised when she had a baby girl four days later. Neither was Mama surprised when Peter broke off his engagement to Penelope. Now that Catherine had a new look outside, Peter was willing to spend time with her and soon appreciated what she was like inside. I wasn't sure he really deserved her, but she confided to me that she had loved him all along.

My baby sister Minnie was just learning how to sit up when Peter and Catherine were married. Penelope didn't come to the reception.

*Sometime around 1880, Peter Greaves Jr. was engaged to a girl not suited to his mother's taste. A lovely girl named Catherine Mortensen came to help with the housekeeping, and Peter's mother Elizabeth took such a liking to her that she arranged to send her to Salt Lake City to become a lady. On Catherine's return, a reluctant Peter was sent to pick her up from the train station. He was distracted from his errand by a beautiful young lady in a red plumed hat. Upon investigation, he was astonished to discover that the fetching young woman was Catherine. They were married on October 9, 1882, and lived happily ever after, according to family historian Winona Erickson.*

*Three-year-old Roy Greaves died in May of 1882. His baby sister Minnie was born a month later, in June of 1882.*

# ARM'S LENGTH

For twenty-five years my grandfather's warning had served me well. "Clive," he'd said to me as he leaned forward in his big armchair by the fire. "The only reason us married men are married is because we couldn't run fast enough. Keep those women at arm's length."

Being a sheepherder made it easy to take Grandpa's advice to heart. I remained a contented bachelor until that fateful day when I first saw Elise Roberts. After that, it was like she had a sheep's crook around my neck, dragging my thoughts around with her.

It happened on my supply run into town. I wasn't looking for love or trouble, when the shop door opened and a brown-eyed girl with freckles sprinkled across the tops of her cheeks came sashaying in. Her brown hair was shot through with dusky red lights as warm as campfire embers. Her hair was pinned up on her head, but one section had escaped, trailing over her shoulder like shining filaments of fishing line. When she turned her head to talk to the pale blonde girl beside her, the curl at the end of the errant strand moved against her bodice like bait on a hook. The lure was irresistible. I wanted this girl wrapped in my arms instead of at arm's length. I couldn't tear my eyes away as she wandered over to the dry goods, exclaiming to her friend over the red calico fabric.

I saw Mr. Braithwaite grinning around his moustache when I finally forced myself to turn around. He pushed the supply slip across the counter for me to sign. I could feel my face heat up, and longed to get out of there. At the same time, I dreaded the thought of leaving.

"Elise," Mr. Braithwaite called, as I scribbled my name. I began piling cans and sacks of sugar and flour into my canvas bag.

"Yes?" a voice as soft and fresh as wind through the aspen leaves caressed my ears. Without any will of my own, I turned to see brown eyes regarding me with what I both hoped and feared was an interested gleam.

"I've got some new yellow gingham I didn't put out yet. Do you want to see it?" Mr. Braithwaite said.

The dusting of freckles lifted as a heart-stopping smile spread across Elise's face. "I surely would," she answered Mr. Braithwaite while looking at me.

"Would you excuse us, Clive?" Mr. Braithwaite said. I nodded mutely.

"Excuse me, Clive," Elise said boldly, tossing me a glance out of the corners of her eyes as she brushed past me much closer than she needed to. I watched her follow Mr. Braithwaite into the storage room. A smell like sunflowers billowed out behind her, and I breathed it in, holding it as long as I could, willing it to seep into my insides and become a part of me.

Elise's face stayed with me all the way back to the sheep camp, her face and that long reddish brown curl with a crook on the end like a beckoning finger urging me closer. I didn't even notice Jeff until I practically rode my horse on top of him. "What's wrong with you?" he yelled as he jumped back in alarm.

I focused on his sunburned face, the lines beside his mouth dark with dirt, his head tipped sideways in curiosity as his shapeless hat brim fluttered in the canyon breeze. "Nothin'," I answered innocently.

Jeff searched my face. "Looks like you went and dipped your tongue into the sugar bag," he mused. "You better not have, though, or else I won't save you any when I go for supplies next month."

My heart jerked away from its dreamy thoughts of Elise and jumped up in defense. "You can't go," I blurted, without even thinking.

Jeff's eyes narrowed. "It's my turn," he said slowly.

My mind cast about for some logical answer to deflect his statement. "You can have the next two turns in a row," I said. "I've got to go back next month."

"Why?" Jeff asked, crossing his arms over his chest.

"I've just got to," I said stupidly.

"What's wrong?" Jeff said.

I grasped at the straw he'd extended me. "Medical reasons," I said. "Heart problems."

"You're too young," Jeff countered, his face a mask of disbelief.

"Tell that to my heart," I said.

Jeff didn't give in right away. When it became clear to him that I was not myself, he began to relent. He'd catch me staring into space with a faraway look in my eye. I'd forget things that used to come automatically to me, and I didn't eat as much as I used to. I daydreamed a lot, imagining Elise beside me, looking out over the flocks and snuggling together on the bluffs at the end of the day as we watched the sunset together. The month between supply runs became tortuously long, seeming to last a year.

When the magical day came, Jeff was so worried about my heart that he practically insisted that I go. As I climbed up on my horse, he said, "Clive, is there a cure?"

"I hope so," I answered as I turned the horse to the trail and hurried him down the mountain. I made a beeline for Brathwaite's store, so intent on my destination that I wasn't looking to either side as I rode into town.

"Hello, Clive." The feminine voice was unmistakable.

I reined in and my poor horse stopped so suddenly he almost sat down. I patted his neck in apology as I stared into the yard beside the Claridge Hotel. Elise was holding a pair of long under-wear in one hand and a clothespin in the other. She stood under-neath a clothesline, a white apron covering her red calico dress. Her smouldery red hair was piled haphazardly on her head with several long, damp tendrils trailing down her back and over her shoulders.

She flung the long johns over the line and swayed toward me. "I haven't seen you for a long time," she said, "Where've you been?"

"Herding sheep," I replied, counting myself lucky that my tongue didn't twist itself into a knot.

"All by yourself?" Elise asked, looking up at me from under-neath her lashes.

"With Jeff," I answered.

"And who's Jeff?" Elise put her elbows up on the pole fence and rested her face on both of her palms. "Is Jeff the loyal and faithful sheep dog?"

"No, he's a guy," I said.

"Are you married?" Elise asked, tipping her head sideways onto one palm as she raised the other to shade her eyes from the sun.

My heart jumped at the question. "No, Ma'am," I answered quickly.

"Climb on down, would you?" Elise said. "The sun's in my eyes when I look up at you like this." I got down off my horse and moved over to the fence. Elise smelled faintly of sweet, dried hay.

"Do you want to be married?" Elise asked suddenly, her brown eyes so dark I couldn't see where the pupil ended and the iris began. My heart jumped into my throat, blocking my ability to speak. Elise put both forearms flat on top of the pole fence, leaning forward on them until her face was close enough to kiss. "Do you want to marry me?" she asked softly.

I heard an echo of Grandfather's voice saying 'run!' just before I heard myself say "Yes." My mouth touched Elise's and my heart melted into my toes. When we broke apart, I saw Elise smiling up at me, and thought I'd never be happier. My arms were aching to hold her when a sudden thought struck me. "What about your parents?" I asked. "They aren't going to let you marry a sheepherder just down off the mountain that you've only seen twice."

Elise's smile turned mischievous. "I'm an orphan," she said, "and I do know you. I asked Mr. Braithwaite about you, and Mrs. Siddons."

"My schoolteacher?" I said, my mouth open wide enough for a flock of sheep to fit into.

"And Mr. Hewlitt, and Mr. Bonacre. Henry and Ethel Carson had something to say about you, too." Elise was positively glowing.

"You must have talked to the whole town," I said, rubbing my forehead and thinking hard if there was anything bad that any of those people might have said.

Elise shrugged her shoulders and the tendrils of hair shifted languidly on her red calico sleeves. "Once I saw you, I wanted to know all about you. I couldn't find you anywhere, or else I would have asked you," she said simply. I didn't know how to argue with that.

"Once I get supplies, I have to head on back to camp," I said.

"How long will it take to get supplies?" she asked.

I gazed toward the mountains and tried to look wise. "Well, I'll stay over tonight so I'm not heading back in the dark. There are wild animals on the prowl up there after dark." I glanced at Elise to see if she was impressed. She was. "I imagine it will take me a couple of hours to round up what I need. I'll stay overnight in town, then head back at first light." I knew tomorrow would come too soon, but it was the best I could do.

"Where will you stay?" Elise asked.

I shrugged. "They usually let me sleep in the hayloft at the stable."

"Stay in the hotel tonight," Elise said, smiling until her freckles begged to be kissed.

I rubbed one of my ears as it grew warm. I hoped my face wasn't following suit. "Don't know that I have the means for that right now," I said.

"Oh, you won't have to pay," Elise said. "Bert and Sally Johnson run the place. I work for them, you see, and they'll be happy to let us have a room for our wedding night. It will be their gift to me."

My eyes about left my head as I stared at Elise. "Our wedding night?" I said, "Tonight?"

Elise wet her lips with her tongue before she answered, "You said yourself that you wanted to marry me. Why wait? You're leaving tomorrow, and I want to go with you." Her slightly parted lips were soft and full, her heated brown eyes searched my face before she said softly, "You haven't changed your mind, have you?"

My thoughts raced. I'd never seriously entertained the thought of getting married at all. Sheep herding was a solitary occupation. If I did get married, I'd imagined long talks with the parents, evenings on a porch swing, and supervised walks. I'd never thought of marrying someone after two meetings, but after all, why not? Who was to say the long way was the right way? Elise was all I'd thought about day and night in the sheep camp. Thoughts of her had entwined themselves around my life like ivy on a garden wall. She must have had similar feelings, since she had talked to everyone who ever knew me. It was flattering that in spite of all she'd heard, she still wanted to marry me. And I wanted to marry her. What difference did it make if we got married today or next year?

I focused on Elise's face. Her bottom lip was thrust slightly forward, the corners of her mouth turned down as her eyes regarded me solemnly. I put my finger under her chin and said, "No, I haven't changed my mind. Do you think Johnson's would throw in a hot bath along with the room?" Although my voice was casual, my heart was beating wildly.

"Yes!" Elise threw her arms around my neck, pulled me across the pole fence, and kissed my cheek. Then she turned and ran for the hotel. The long johns on the clothesline waited patiently for someone to come and hang them straight. I climbed back on my horse and rode to the store, feeling as though my horse was walking on a cushiony cloud.

"What's wrong with you, Clive?" Mr. Braithwaite asked me right off.

"I'm getting married," I said, the words sounding strange, yet exhilarating.

Mr. Braithwaite raised his hand to his mouth and rubbed his moustache thoughtfully. "Elise?" he asked.

The sound of her name put a catch in my heart. "Yes, Sir," I said.

"Well, you could do worse," he said. "She's a spunky girl. Don't you go abusing her heart."

I wasn't used to the stern look in his eye. "No, Sir," I said stoutly.

Mr. Braithwaite smiled. "I had a feeling about you two. Congratulations."

"Thank you, Sir," I said. Before long, the supplies were all gathered and piled on the counter. Mr. Braithwaite reached out to the shelf behind him and picked up a paper wrapped square. He set it on top of the supply stack. Puzzled, I looked at him, then the paper square, then back at him.

"Soap," he said.

I checked the list in my hand. "I don't think..." I began, but Mr. Braithwaite interrupted me.

"Wedding gift," he said, and winked. My face got uncomfortably hot, and I rubbed a spot on my jaw that didn't even itch.

"Thank you," I said, not knowing what else to say.

I secured the supplies on my horse, and headed for the hotel. As I pulled into the yard, I noticed that someone had hung Mr. Long Johns straight and proper, and the laundry basket had been taken in. Heart beating hard, I got my horse settled in the barn, had a hot bath with the soap from Mr. Braithwaite, then got dressed with my extra shirt which I kept rolled up in my saddle blanket. I found my way to the parlor. A thin man watched me enter, scrutinizing my progress through a pair of small round glasses straddling the bridge of his nose. He put his hand out toward me. "Clive?" I nodded. "Bert Johnson," he introduced himself. He cleared his throat. "Elise is like family," he said. Then he clasped his hands behind his back and stared down at the floor for a moment. He raised his head and looked me in the eye. "You take care of her," he said.

"Yes, Sir," I said solemnly. I hadn't planned to do anything different. I wouldn't dare, with Mr. Braithwaite and Mr. Johnson to answer to. I swallowed hard as a lump of uncertainty rose in my throat. Was I doing the right thing?

Female voices sounded in the hall behind me. Elise and a pudgy woman with a tearful smile and hair the color of dirt came bustling into the room. I assumed that the woman was Sally Johnson, but I didn't give her more than a fleeting thought. Elise had on a dress of sunny white and yellow gingham. The full skirt was gathered in at the waist, and the bodice fitted her like my favorite old glove molded itself to my hand. Her hair was pinned up proper, with no naughty strands escaping to brush the sides of her face or dance unchecked down her back. Her smile was warm and shy, and my uncertainty melted off me like snow in a room with a fireplace fire going full blast.

After the preacher married us in a simple ceremony punctuated by Mrs. Johnson's sniffles, we had a chicken dinner prepared by Mrs. Johnson that I'm sure was good, but I don't remember it very well. Afterward, Elise and I made our way up to our room and closed the door behind us.

I felt mighty proud the next morning riding out of town with my pretty wife on the horse behind me. Her arms were wrapped around my waist as snug as a belt, but they felt much better than any belt I'd ever worn. At times Elise exclaimed about the scenery, or an animal that she saw scuttle into the undergrowth. When she wasn't talking, she laid her head on my back and snuggled in like she was meant to be there.

As we pulled into camp, Jeff hailed me. "Clive! What'd the doc say? Are you all right?"

"I'm cured," I said, twisting around to take Elise's arm and help her slide down the side of the horse. "This is the best medicine anyone ever prescribed for me."

Elise found her balance on the ground and giggled, "Oh, Clive!"

Jeff stared as though he'd forgotten how to blink. "This is Elise," I said as I dismounted.

Elise did a little curtsy thing and said, "Pleased to meet you."

"Clive! Are you crazy? You can't bring a girl up here!" Jeff hollered.

"This girl is my wife," I answered smugly, pleased in some perverse way to see the shock ripple across Jeff's face as his mouth went slack. "Where are your manners?" I chided Jeff as I put my arm protectively around Elise. "You should at least greet her before you shout at me."

Jeff whipped his hat off. "Sorry, Ma'am," he mumbled to Elise as his ears and cheekbones colored as red as sunburn. Plopping his hat back on his head, he said with more control in his voice, "Why didn't you tell me, Clive?"

"I didn't know myself," I said reasonably. "It was Elise's idea, and it seemed like a good one."

"Well, I never," Jeff said, but forgot to say what it was he "nevered."

We made arrangements for Jeff to sleep in a tent, and Elise and I took over the camp wagon. We bunked together on a bed, which was unfortunately not as big as the one at the hotel. Elise wasn't used to the aspen pole base, either. She piled blankets over the mattress until she couldn't feel the poles anymore. Her bed at the hotel had been supported by criss-crossed ropes with some "give" in them. The aspen poles were straight and stiff and tied together with rawhide.

Things went along just fine for a week or so. Elise sat by me on the bluff overlooking the sheep and the sunset after she'd cooked us some mighty good supper, a lot better than Jeff or I ever grubbed up. Every night Elise snuggled with me on our aspen pole bed, nestling in the hollow of my shoulder, her arm thrown across my chest, her hair tickling my chin, and I wondered at my good fortune.

Yet after I started bunking with Elise, I found that I wasn't getting the sleep I was used to. I woke up several times in the night, but not because of coyotes howling or a warning bark from the sheep dogs. I wasn't used to someone else in my bed. Sometimes my arm would go to sleep, all numb and lifeless from Elise's head lying on it too long. Sometimes I'd roll over and find Elise in my way. Sometimes her hair would get in my face and give me nightmares of suffocating in my horse's mane. I was reveling in the closeness of my affectionate wife, but suffering from lack of sleep.

I had to do something, but I didn't want to hurt Elise's feelings. After all, she needed a place to sleep, too, and I'd rather have her for a bunkmate than Jeff. I pondered on the matter some, until I finally hit on a solution that I hoped would work.

I began one afternoon when Elise was down at the river washing clothes. I didn't want her to see what I was doing and think it was because I didn't love her. I flung back the covers and mattress on our bed, exposing the aspen poles. Taking my pocketknife, I cut the leather thongs that bound the poles. With some new leather strips, I pulled in the two center poles, cinching them as tightly as Elise held me in the night. I wrapped and tied the new leather thongs around the rest of the poles, adjusting the spacing to compensate for new arrangement. When I heard footsteps outside, I barely had time to fling the mattress and blankets back into place before Elise pushed a wicker basket into the small camp wagon ahead of her. She stopped when she saw me, a delighted smile spreading across her face.

"Clive! I thought you'd be out with the sheep!"

A niggle of guilt in my stomach made me squirm. "I'd better go take my turn from Jeff," I said. "I just wanted to see what we were havin' for supper."

"Mutton," Elise said, setting down the basket and moving over in front of me. She wrapped her arms around my waist and pressed her freckled cheek against my shirt. I couldn't help but wrap my arms around her. She lifted her face to smile at me, and I lowered my face to kiss her.

That night, after Elise fell asleep, the slight ridge formed by the two poles in the middle of our bed made her roll over against the wagon's wall. I slept soundly, dreaming of little freckle-faced girls and dusky red-haired boys running and playing underneath a clothesline full of long johns.

*According to James Jacobs of Ogden, Utah, an unnamed sheep-herder got married in the early 1900's. He took his new bride to sheep camp with him so they could enjoy a honeymoon while he earned a salary at the same time. Used to sleeping alone, the sheepherder had a hard time getting a good night's rest in the arms of his new bride. He solved the problem by tightening the aspen poles in the center of the bed, thus creating a ridge that rolled his affectionate wife over to her own side of the mattress after she fell asleep at night.*

# BETTER LATE THAN NEVER

Diana was walking toward me down the street, dabbing at her eyes with a damp handkerchief. "Now what?" I asked impatiently.

Diana stopped and glanced up at me with surprised eyes forming little circles of blue. "Mary! I didn't see you!" she mumbled from behind her handkerchief.

"That's no surprise," I retorted. For a nineteen-year-old, she sure could cry like a baby.

"Do you know Martha Sorenson?" Diana asked, gesturing behind her with one arm. I looked past her and saw a little old woman in a long gray dress shuffling away from us.

"Of course I know her," I said.

"But do you know her sad story?" Diana asked as a fresh wash of tears spilled down her cheeks. She blotted at them with the limp handkerchief.

I rolled my eyes before I said, "Everyone has a sad story."

"But this," Diana's chin quivered before she could go on, "is the saddest I've ever heard."

"Must have something to do with lost love," I said flippantly, my heart pained from my own disappointing love as my face remained stony.

"But he wasn't lost!" Diana said earnestly. "He was just too late!"

"It happens," I said, thinking of my own life. What if I had come to Utah the same time Elder Carpenter did? Would my story have a different ending?

I turned to walk beside Diana as we made our way to the Ray's house. I was staying with Diana's cousin Corinda Ray because I had no other home. My parents were living in my native country of Hungary. When I begged to come to America, my uncle in Cincinnati agreed to sponsor me. After my baptism and my unrealized plan to marry Elder Carpenter, I decided to move to Utah where I could live in the midst of more church members. Now here I was, twenty-one years old, living in Salt Lake City and earning my keep as nanny for the Rays.

"You know she's Norwegian," Diana said.

"You mean Martha?"

Diana nodded as she blew her nose. "When she joined the church in Norway, she was turned out of house and home."

"Like so many others," I interjected, not seeing why Diana would pity Martha in particular.

"But not like all the others," Diana said firmly. "Her fiancée met her at the boat dock, just at the very moment she was going to board the ship." My throat got tight when I heard the word "fiancée," so I didn't reply. The man I had wanted as my fiancée had married another woman.

Diana darted her eyes sideways at me. "He told her that if she would give up her church membership, he would still marry her, because he loved her so much."

Diana choked up again while my heart encased itself in a self-protective layer of ice. I steered Diana around the corner onto the street where we lived. "At least she got a choice," I said callously, knowing what Martha had chosen because, after all, she was here.

"She wouldn't give up the gospel," Diana informed me unnecessarily. "She got on the boat only to barely survive the journey across the ocean. After that, she had to walk all the way here." Diana's chin thrust forward as though she had her sights set on the west, determined to get through no matter what.

"Like so many others," I said impatiently.

Diana's voice rose almost to a shout. "But then she got married to old Brother Sorenson. She was his third wife, you know."

"I know, I know," I answered.

Diana turned her face toward me, her hands held out in supplication. "She was assigned to marry him," she said as though it was the worst punishment meted out in life.

"It's happened before," I answered. "She could have said no."

"But she had to marry somebody," Diana insisted.

My temper flared. "Why?" I asked, with more belligerence than I intended.

Diana stared over at me in utter disbelief. "To get to the Celestial Kingdom," she said, shaking her head a little as though she couldn't believe anyone would not be born knowing that. I had the sudden urge to push Diana's smug, self-righteous face into a mud puddle, but it hadn't rained recently. More's the pity.

"Girls, what are you quarreling about?" The soft voice of Corinda Ray at her front door made me jump guiltily.

"Doesn't everyone have to get married?" Diana asked as she strode inside, "Whether they choose the husband or the husband is chosen for them?" She plopped down on the sofa. I followed her and sat stiffly on the opposite side of the couch from her.

Corinda eyed us with surprise as she lowered herself into a chair. "Are you just asking about women? What about men?"

Diana looked confused. "Well, of course men get married."

"Some of them used to get married a lot," I said mockingly, my eyes wide with pretended ignorance.

"Whom are you talking about?" Corinda asked as she folded her arms.

Diana answered, "Martha Sorenson."

Corinda nodded knowingly. She lowered her eyes to the ground for a moment before she looked at Diana and said, "We always have a choice. Martha did what she thought was right."

"But when her Norwegian beau couldn't forget her, he followed her all the way to Salt Lake City."

"He's not the first one," I reminded Diana. She ignored me.

"Just imagine," Diana said earnestly to Corinda, correctly assuming that she'd found a more sympathetic audience. "He followed her half way around the world because he loved her so much, and couldn't live without her. He found her in Salt Lake City just before she was leaving for a new settlement." A tear escaped over her eyelashes and ran down her cheek. "But she was already married to Brother Sorenson."

Corinda surveyed the distraught face of her cousin with compassion. "Life is full of choices," she said softly.

The ice shield had cracked and my heart was swelling dangerously close to pain, so I said abruptly, "She could have divorced Brother Sorenson and married her young man."

"Break her vows?" Diana said, turning to me with fire in her eyes.

I shrugged. "Brother Sorenson had two other wives. It's not like she would have been leaving him all alone."

"You can't understand the sanctity of marriage vows since you've never been married," Diana said in her superior-to-you voice.

"Oh, and you have?" I said sharply.

"Girls," Corinda said in mild reproach.

Diana's next words stabbed me to the heart, although she didn't mean for them to. "Thomas asked me to marry him. We were going to wait and be sealed in the temple when he got over his Word of Wisdom problem, but I can't wait now, after hearing Martha's story. Too many things could go wrong. I'm going to tell him we've got to get married right away."

"Oh, Diana, I'm so happy for you," Corinda stood and leaned over to embrace her cousin. "Thomas is a fine young man, in spite of his tobacco habit. You will be good for each other, and he will overcome."

Corinda threw a glance at me. "Congratulations, Di," I said, pushing up from the couch. "I'll go get some kindling," I volunteered as I hurried away from talk of weddings and happily-ever-afters.

Walking through the house toward the back door, I heard Michael twisting in his bed. When I peeked in at him, he caught my eye and smiled so big that it covered half his face. "Hey, Minkle," I said, scooping him up and swinging him against my shoulder. Corinda's youngest child felt as much my own as anyone could. Michael's brother Gabriel came racing into the room at the sound of my voice and wrapped his arms around my legs, making it difficult to walk. "Hey, Brave Gabe," I exclaimed. "You're getting so big and strong, you'd better not squeeze my legs off."

Gabriel giggled delightedly and let go, a miniature storm running out of the room as only a three-year-old could. Since I had Michael in my arms, I was glad that Gabriel hurried ahead of me to the woodpile and helped carry in two handfuls of kindling.

The next day I was not the least bit surprised to hear that Thomas agreed there was no sense putting off the wedding. He fervently promised that he would quit his tobacco habit. His father had already given him the old two-room house they'd built when they first came into the valley. The family had long since moved into a bigger house, built to accommodate all of Tom's younger brothers and sisters. Now Tom only had to clear out the grain that was being stored in the old house. It took him just a couple of days to sweep it clean and get a bed set up in one room for him and Diana.

Tom's family decided that with all the work on the farm, they wouldn't be able to make the long journey to the courthouse for the civil wedding. Corinda didn't feel up to traveling with Gabriel and Michael, especially since the county seat was far enough away that they'd have to stay overnight. There was no way I was going to go see Diana get married when my heart was still hurting from my own lost love. So Diana and Thomas set off together in a buggy, the fee for their wedding license folded securely in Thomas's wallet. I wondered if the wife of whichever Bishop married them would help Diana cry through the ceremony.

Thomas and Diana returned the next day just at dusk. I wasn't in any hurry to go visit Diana in her blissful domesticity, and she didn't seem to be anxious to come see us right away, either. Corinda seemed content to leave Diana to her own housekeeping. We spent a week or so adjusting to a routine around Diana's absence and keeping busy with the boys.

Still, I couldn't avoid Diana forever. One day a light knock sounded on the door just before it opened to admit Diana, who was smiling and pink-cheeked. I gazed on her with longing, imagining myself in her place, had Gerald not broken my heart. Yet in scrutinizing the days that led to my conversion, I had to admit that Elder Gerald Carpenter had never promised me marriage. On the day I joined the church, I was filled with warmth from my burning testimony, and when Elder Carpenter raised his hands and blessed the water for baptism, my heart lurched with conviction as the words, "There's my man!" came unbidden into my head. When I found out he'd returned to Utah after his mission and married a woman named Bertella, I berated myself for mistaking butterflies in my stomach for a heavenly message. I determined to put Elder Carpenter out of my mind. I traveled to Salt Lake City, met Corinda, and was content with our arrangement of earning room and board in exchange for helping with her two boys until her husband returned from his mission. But now, looking at Diana's countenance, the longing for a happy marriage loomed large and unwelcome in my heart.

"You're looking radiant!" Corinda greeted Diana with a one-armed hug as she balanced Michael on her hip. "Married life suits you!"

"It's wonderful!" Diana gushed. "Thomas hasn't had a single chaw of tobacco since our wedding day! He's kept his promise!"

There was too much bliss in the air for my taste, so I said unnecessarily, "Two rooms isn't much for a house."

"It's enough for us," Diana quickly assured me, before she blushed. "At least for now." I felt my stomach flip over with jealousy.

Corinda glanced at me. "Will you take Michael and wash his hands and face, please?" she said. I reached for the little boy as Corinda asked Diana, "How was the wedding, dear?" I didn't really want to hear, but as I tucked Michael into my arms, I felt a tug of curiosity that made me walk slowly toward the kitchen door.

"Easy!" Diana beamed, obviously proud that they had accomplished the first step in their lives together all by themselves.

Corinda persisted for details. "Who married you?"

"Oh, I don't know his name. He was the clerk in the courthouse." Diana waved her hand dismissively. "He signed the license, though. I could go get it for you if you really want to know."

Corinda tipped her head. "Didn't you get a bishop to marry you?"

Diana's forehead creased in thought. "No. They never told us to."

Corinda was silent for a moment before she said slowly, "So you went to the courthouse and got your license and then you came back?"

Diana looked down at the floor and admitted, "Well, it was too late to come right back, so we did stay at a hotel." Her cheeks pinked up again, as though she'd been standing too long over a hot stove. "We came home the next day."

"And you never saw a Bishop?" Corinda asked again.

Diana narrowed her eyes and looked closely at Corinda's face. "I already said we didn't. Is something wrong?"

"I'm afraid that if all you did was go to the courthouse and pay for your marriage license, you're not legally married," Corinda said apologetically.

Diana's mouth opened silently as her face paled. Her hand clutched the neckline of her dress before she whispered, "Not married?"

"I don't think so," Corinda said gently. Diana covered her mouth with her hand, her eyes now round and horrified.

"Mary, never mind about Michael. Go see if you can find Bishop Jacobs. Diana, do you want me to get Thomas?"

Diana lowered her hand and whispered miserably, "We didn't know."

Corinda put her arm around Diana and said, "I know you didn't. I suppose one of us should have gone with you. The bishop will understand. We just need to take care of it as soon as possible."

I left Corinda trying to console Diana. It took me awhile to find Bishop Jacobs, and when I did, I found that I was embarrassed to tell him what the situation was. I managed to stutter through it, and after a quiet pause, he asked me to have Thomas and Diana meet him at his house that evening.

I went back home and gave Corinda the message. "Will you stay with the boys?" she asked me, "or do you want to go to the wedding?"

"I'll stay," I assured her quickly. Even though I hadn't been exactly charitable to Diana, I wasn't interested in seeing her embarrassed further.

After Corinda led an unusually quiet Diana outside, I got busy making a snack for the boys before we settled down with a story-book. I'd only read the first two pages when a knock sounded at the door. I scooted Gabriel off my lap and hoisted Michael onto my hip. I opened the door to find a young woman who looked vaguely familiar. She smiled and said, "Is this the Ray residence?"

"Yes, but they aren't home," I replied. As hard as I tried, I couldn't place her. "May I take your name?"

The young woman nodded. "I'm Edith Carpenter. I'm look-ing for Mary Koch."

Her words had the curious effect of warming my heart and making the back of my neck prickle at the same time. The name "Carpenter" played itself over and over in my head like children chanting in a schoolyard. "Why are you looking for me?" I asked.

"So you're Mary?" Edith asked, her eyes brightening. I nodded. Edith tipped her head questioningly. "Are these your children?"

"Oh, no!" I answered. "I'm their nanny." I could feel my face heat up uncomfortably before I blurted, "I'm not even married."

Edith nodded and smiled. "I'm here because our family has heard such good things about you from Gerald, and I wanted to meet you. I'm his sister. May I come in?"

"Yes, of course," I answered, stepping back quickly and bump-ing into Gabriel.

"Ow, ow, ow!" he hollered, plopping down on his behind and grabbing his foot in his little hands.

"Oh, Gabe, I'm so sorry!" I said, bending and putting my arms around the little boy. "Come sit on my lap, and let me see."

With acting ability beyond his years, Gabriel limped into the parlor. I sat down and propped Michael up against my side. Gabriel climbed into my lap. Edith had followed and sat in the armchair opposite us. She watched as I pulled off Gabriel's shoe and sock and rubbed his foot, assuring myself that there really was

SHIRLEY BAHLMANN

nothing broken. Just so Gabriel would feel I was taking him seriously, I wrapped a large strip of fabric around his foot. Delighted, the little boy stood and walked on the heel of his "injured" foot, keeping the bandage up in the air as he stumped around the room. "Wait'll Mama sees this!" he said.

"Yes, I can hardly wait," I said, twisting my mouth into a rueful smile.

Edith claimed my attention when she said, "Mother and Father are most anxious to meet you. Would you consider coming for a visit?"

My mouth fell open with shock before I got control of it and said, "Me? Why?"

Edith smiled warmly, "As I said, Gerald has only praised you. He thinks you were terribly brave to come to America by yourself, and he was touched by how eagerly you embraced the gospel. He also says you are very kind-hearted." I thought of Diana and felt a twinge of guilt. "My parents would dearly love to meet you," Edith said earnestly. When I didn't answer, Edith turned her head theatrically from side to side as though checking for eavesdroppers. Then she leaned closer to me and confided, "Mother says you were a good influence on Gerald." Edith leaned back and clasped her hands together. She stared at her interlocked fingers, then shrugged her shoulders. "Call it curiosity if you like, or call it the mothering instinct. My mother is not well, or she would have come to meet you herself. It would mean a lot to her if you would come." Edith raised her eyes to mine. She must have read the hesitation my heart had put there, because she leaned over and put a gentle hand on my knee. "Besides, I can see that everything Gerald said is true. I like you even though I've just met you," she assured me. "You have a good heart, and a good sense of humor." Her eyes cut over to Gabriel who was experimenting with spinning in slow circles on his bandaged foot. "You'll like my parents. Please come."

Her eyes pulled at my heart. They were so like Gerald's. I heard myself accepting the invitation, feeling warmed and secure in the belief that Edith truly did like me. Edith left soon afterward. The boys were asleep in their beds when Corinda returned from the wedding. She was alone.

131

"Oh, Mary, you're a treasure," she said as she sank down onto the sofa. "Thanks for taking care of things while I was gone."

"How was the wedding?" I asked.

"Sad," Corinda admitted. "Poor Diana couldn't seem to forgive herself." Corinda closed her eyes and rubbed her forehead with one hand. "Bishop Jacobs was very kind. I'm sure he'll help them through. They'll make it to the temple yet."

"I've been invited to visit the Carpenters," I blurted out.

Corinda opened her eyes and looked at me with her brow furrowed. "The Carpenters?"

"You know, Elder Carpenter taught me the gospel in Cincinnati," I said.

"You're going to see him?" Corinda sat up and looked at me warily.

"His parents. I may not even see him at all," I said. After I explained the situation, Corinda surprised me by encouraging my impromptu holiday.

A week later, I found myself riding the train into the station at the end of my journey. I turned my gaze to the window, scanning the faces to see if I could spot Edith. My heart jumped when I recognized Gerald's face in the crowd. The warmth that spread through me at the unexpected sight of him wasn't even quelled when I noticed Gerald bend down and speak to a pretty young woman at his side who had a toddler balanced on her hip. The baby was wearing a bonnet and had a finger in her mouth.

As soon as I stepped off the train, I heard Gerald speak my name. He approached me with a broad smile. One of his arms went around me in a quick hug just before the other picked up my suitcase. He stepped back, his face beaming. "Mary! I'm so glad you came! This is my wife, Bertella, and my daughter, Julie."

"Hello, Mary," Bertella said warmly as she leaned over to hug me. Up close, Julie's blue eyes searched mine for a serious moment before she decided to smile at me around her finger. My heart melted as I felt their love reach out and embrace me.

Gerald and Bertella took me to his parents' house. He led the way into the parlor where his mother was sitting in an overstuffed chair. "Mother, this is Mary," Gerald said as proudly as if he was presenting a fancy birthday cake he'd made himself.

Matilda Carpenter pulled herself to her feet before she put both arms around me. "Oh, Mary, I am delighted to meet you!"

Two boys came thundering in from the hallway. When they saw me, they stopped suddenly, the smaller one skidding on a throw rug. "Boys!" Matilda reproached them. "Come and meet Mary like gentlemen." Her voice was stern, but I saw that Matilda's eyes were full of love.

The older boy, who looked to be about twelve years old, stepped toward me with his hand out on the end of an arm as stiff as a pump handle. "Pleased to meet you," he said, "I'm Edwin."

"Pleased to meet you, too, Edwin," I said as I took his hand. Edwin ducked his head and stepped back awkwardly, his cheeks blooming dark pink.

The smaller boy, eight or nine years old, suddenly stuck his hand out toward me as though he was anxious to get the ordeal over with as soon as possible. "I'm George," he declared.

"Hello, George," I said, taking the slightly sticky hand. "You're quite a gentleman." George's skinny little chest puffed out and his face turned up into a pleased grin as he pulled his hand out of mine.

A handsome man with graying hair appeared in the doorway. "Dad, this is Mary. Mary, my father, Joseph," Gerald announced.

"Hello, Mary," Joseph Carpenter greeted me, turning his hand-shake into a quick hug. "We're so glad you came." Joseph took his arm from me and put it around his wife. "Matilda, you need to sit down," he said gently. For the first time, I noticed Matilda squint-ing as though her eyes had something in them. She tottered as her husband helped her ease into her chair. "George, get your mother a drink of water," he told the boy. George dashed off to do as he was asked.

"Are you all right?" I asked Matilda, concerned over her appar-ent discomfort.

"The doctors say I have diabetes," Matilda said. "I must admit, some days are better than others, but having you here makes this a very good day." The warmth of her words made me glad that I had come.

The three days of my visit felt like three minutes. I was torn as I rode the train back toward Salt Lake City. Part of my heart was at the Carpenter's house, but Corinda still needed me. I had promised Matilda that after Brother Ray's return home from his mission in the spring, I would come back and help her with her two half-grown boys. She admitted that she wasn't able to chase them around like she had her older children since her legs often suffered from numbness and tingling. I already felt like part of the family, and didn't want Matilda to worry needlessly about her boys. Edwin and George reminded me of Gabriel and Michael, only they were bigger and had a larger vocabulary.

I eagerly greeted the little Ray boys as soon as I stepped through the door, sitting down to snuggle them both on my lap as I told Corinda about my visit.

"Mary, you are positively glowing," she said. "You really should go back to help Matilda Carpenter."

"I don't need to go right now," I replied stoutly as I rocked the two boys slowly back and forth. "What would I do without my Minkle and Brave Gabe? I'll wait until spring."

"All right," Corinda said. "I must admit, the selfish part of me is glad."

I sent the Carpenters a thank you note, and they answered me promptly, assuring me that I was welcome at any time. I easily fell back into my usual routine, although my thoughts often returned to the Carpenters. I wondered how Matilda was getting along. Some days spring seemed to be far away.

One day Corinda handed me a letter from Matilda. I eagerly tore it open, but after reading the first few lines, my hand flew to my mouth and I couldn't see to read anymore. I tried to wipe the tears from my eyes. "Mary, what's wrong?" Corinda asked as she touched my trembling hand still clutching the letter.

"She died," I choked out.

"Matilda?" Corinda asked softly.

"No. Bertella." With aching heart, I imagined little Julie sitting in a high chair, waiting for her mother to come and feed her, or to gently wipe her messy face and hands before lifting her out to cuddle her and rock her to sleep. She couldn't know that her mother would never come back. I put both hands to my face, the letter crumpled between my fingers. I cried for Julie and Gerald, indeed, for the whole Carpenter family.

Soft little hands on my knee brought my thoughts back to the Rays. "Mawy?" Gabriel asked. The sound of his little voice made me cry harder.

"Come here, son," Corinda said before I felt the little hands pull away from my skirt. "What was it?" Corinda said gently. "How did she die?" I took one hand away from my face and pushed the letter over to Corinda. Then I fished in my sleeve with my fingers until I caught the edge of the handkerchief that I kept tucked in there. I wiped my eyes as Corinda said sadly, "Influenza." After a short pause, she said, "At least the baby survived."

I stared at her in horror. "Julie was sick?"

"No," Corinda shook her head. "It was the infant." She looked at my face, then said, "Maybe you didn't read that far. Bertella died nine hours after giving birth to a baby boy. Matilda asks if you will come to the funeral."

I tried to grasp this new piece of information as I blew my nose. "Of course I'll go," I said stoutly.

"Yes, you must," Corinda said, folding the letter and handing it back to me, her face sober.

"I'll come back afterward," I promised fervently. Corinda merely nodded. I held out my arms to Gabriel and he fell into them, cuddling against my neck for a minute before pulling back and tipping his head questioningly. "Mawy have owie?" he asked, his little face set in serious contemplation.

"Yes, Gabe," I said. "Give me a hug." Gabriel's little arms slid around my neck and I held onto him and let the tears roll down my face unchecked.

I thought I'd cried all I could, but I couldn't stop the tears from surprising me every now and then as I rode the train to my sad destination. It was Edith who met me at the station, her face managing a small smile when she caught sight of me. "How's Gerald?" I asked as I embraced her.

"Trying to understand," Edith said as we pulled apart. Her eyes were moist. "He knows in his head that the Lord allows adversity for reasons unknown to us, but he's still trying to put it in his heart."

We made our way to the Carpenter house, where I was greeted warmly. I wished I could erase the pain of loss that lay under the smiles and hugs, but I didn't know how. Gerald was holding Julie in his arms. The toddler looked uncertain when she saw me, as though trying to figure out where she'd seen me before. "I'm so sorry Gerald," I said, my eyes filling up again.

"Yes. Thank you," Gerald said softly, putting one arm around me while he kept hold of Julie. Julie put her soft baby hand on my cheek, and when I looked at her from the closeness of her father's embrace, she gave me a delighted little smile.

As I greeted Matilda, I noticed a small, white bundle on her lap. "Mary," she said, holding out her arms toward me. I moved into her embrace. The bundle on her lap squirmed and let out a little mew. I pushed back the blanket from the tiny red face and looked at Bertella's infant son. He looked world-weary already; his face squinched up as little wails of distress escaped his mouth.

"Would you like me to hold him for you?" I asked.

"Please," Matilda said. As I scooped up the baby, I noticed that Matilda was sitting in a chair that had wheels on the legs. Startled, my eyes flew back to hers.

"It's all right, Mary," Matilda assured me with a tired smile. "I'm blessed to have a wheeled chair and not have to be dragged behind a horse on an Indian travois! Always remember to count your blessings, not your trials. Now take that baby into the kitchen and give him some milk. There's a good girl." I managed to get a little bit of milk into the baby before he fussed himself into an uneasy sleep.

Bertella's funeral was punctuated with many tears. The mourners connected with frequent hugs, trying to draw comfort from the loved ones they could still touch. When it was over, we returned home where Matilda's husband helped her to bed. She was alarmingly pale and weak. I handed the baby to Gerald and got busy in the kitchen, helping to feed the family that had traveled from out of town for the funeral. When the house finally cleared out, I went to check on Matilda. Edwin was standing awkwardly in the hallway looking uncertainly at his mother's closed door.

"Edwin?" I said. Startled, he turned to face me. "Are you all right?" I asked.

He dropped his eyes and shoved his hands deep in his pockets. He spoke so softly that I had to move closer to hear him. "Is Ma going to die?"

My heart constricted in my chest as I cast about for the right words. "Only God knows," I said softly.

The half grown boy suddenly bent into himself, trying to hide his face from me as he nursed a private misery. Impulsively, I moved to him and wrapped my arms around his shaking shoulders. He was close to being as tall as I was. He felt stiff and bony, resisting my embrace, but I held on. After a few moments, Edwin relaxed into my arms and let his head down, his tears wetting my shoulder. I just held on until I could feel his worst grief ebbing away. Before he pulled back, I said firmly, "I'll bet your mother would like a tall drink of water as soon as she wakes up. It's your job to get it into her room quietly." I glanced up and down the corridor before I whispered to him, "You know George could never do it. Do you accept your assignment?"

Edwin pulled away from me, his wet eyes sparked with determination. "Absolutely," he said, and headed for the kitchen.

I heard a small cry behind me. I turned to see Gerald standing forlornly in the hallway, his disheveled hair and crestfallen face making him look a lot like Edwin, only bigger. He balanced the fussy infant on one arm as Julie hung onto his leg, whining to be picked up. "Mary, I can't get him to take any milk," Gerald said, his eyes shadowed with defeat.

"I'll take him," I said. "You and Julie go sit down. Maybe you could get her to take a nap," I suggested. I hoped that Gerald would fall asleep, too. He looked like he desperately needed some rest.

As I carried the baby into the kitchen, I felt a sense of belonging settle over my heart. I would miss Gabriel and Michael, but Corinda would understand. Brother Ray would be home soon. With the peaceful assurance that comes only from heaven, I knew I had found my place. Gerald and I were married six months later. Although it was not the way I had envisioned when I'd dreamed of love and romance, I had, indeed, found my man.

*Carolyn Bessey tells the story of her great-grandmother, Martha Larsen, who left Norway after she joined the Church of Jesus Christ of Latter Day Saints. Her fiancée met her at the boat dock and begged her to renounce her church membership so that he could marry her. She refused, made the trek to Utah, and accepted the assignment to become the third wife to an older polygamist, Soren Sorensen, in 1863. Just before leaving to settle new territory, her young man from Norway tracked her down in Salt Lake City and pled with her to marry him. Feeling a responsibility for the marriage vows she'd already made, Martha followed her husband and his two wives into the wilderness, leaving her childhood sweetheart behind.*

*In 1978, James L. Jacobs of Ogden, Utah retold the story of when he was a young boy around the turn of the 20th century. He and his sister watched through the window as their father, the bishop, hastily married a young couple who assumed the purchase of their wedding license a few weeks earlier was the only formality they needed to be legally wed.*

*According to Carl Carpenter's account, Mary Koch became acquainted with Elder J. Gerald Carpenter when he helped with her conversion on his mission in Cincinnati in the early 1900's. When he raised his hands over the river and blessed the water at her baptism, she had the distinct feeling that "there was her man." After he returned home, the first word she received of him was that he had married a woman named Bertella. Cut to the quick, Mary resolved to put him out of her mind. She took an opportunity to go to Salt Lake City where there were more members of the church. She got a job as a nanny with the Ray family. Gerald's sister Edith contacted Mary there and asked her to come for a visit. Mary was treated kindly by the Carpenters, so when Gerald's* mother, Matilda, who suffered from diabetes, (at this time insulin hadn't been discovered), asked if she would stay and help her with her two pre-teen sons, Mary agreed to return in the spring. Her plans changed when she got word that Bertella had died from influenza only nine hours after giving birth to a baby boy. Mary went to the funeral and couldn't say no when Matilda asked her to help care for the infant. About six months later, Mary and Gerald were married, and remained sweethearts for fifty-nine years, until Gerald's death in 1978.

The end 2/19/04 IMC

# BIOGRAPHY

Shirley Anderson Bahlmann was born in Logan, Utah, and spent her childhood in Haddon Heights, New Jersey. She is fourth in a family of six girls and two boys, a red-haired mother and a harmonica-playing father.

When she was twelve, her family moved to Manti, Utah. Music, writing, English and drama were her favorite school subjects. She wrote her first novel when she was ten years old. She enjoyed French class in junior high, journalism in high school, and editing the Snow College newspaper during her sophomore year there.

She also kept busy playing saxophone in the jazz band, winning the Miss Snow College crown, and meeting her tall, dark, and handsome husband, Robert.

Over the years she has written road shows, skits, family plays, and freelance material for friends and local newspapers.

Shirley has always had a fascination for old houses, buildings and ghost towns. Being of old pioneer stock, she has a natrual curiosity about the people who actually settled the western United States. She also feels fortunate to have perspective from new pioneers, since her husband is the son of Dutch immigrants.

Shirley and Robert are the proud parents of six sons—Andy, Jeff, Scott, Zackary, Brian, and Michael—whose ages span twenty years. The three youngest still live at home.

Shirley loves to hear from her readers. She can be e-mailed at: **www.shirleybahlmann.com**